Torah Studies

CHAIRMAN
Rabbi Moshe Kotlarsky, OBM

PRINCIPAL BENEFACTOR
Mr. George Rohr

EXECUTIVE DIRECTOR
Rabbi Efraim Mintz

TORAH STUDIES CHAIRMAN
Rabbi Yosef Gansburg

EDITOR
Rabbi Ahrele Loschak

CONTRIBUTING AUTHOR
Rabbi Eliezer Gurkow

ADMINISTRATOR
Rabbi Shlomie Tenenbaum

Printed in USA, 2024
© Published and Copyrighted by
THE ROHR JEWISH LEARNING INSTITUTE
832 Eastern Parkway, Brooklyn, NY 11213
All rights reserved.
No part of the contents of this book
may be reproduced or transmitted
in any form or by any means without
the written permission of the publisher.

(888) YOUR-JLI / (718) 221-6900
WWW.MYJLI.COM

ב"ה

SEASON ONE | 5785
YEAR 20 | BOOK 73

TORAH STUDIES

A WEEKLY JOURNEY INTO THE SOUL OF TORAH

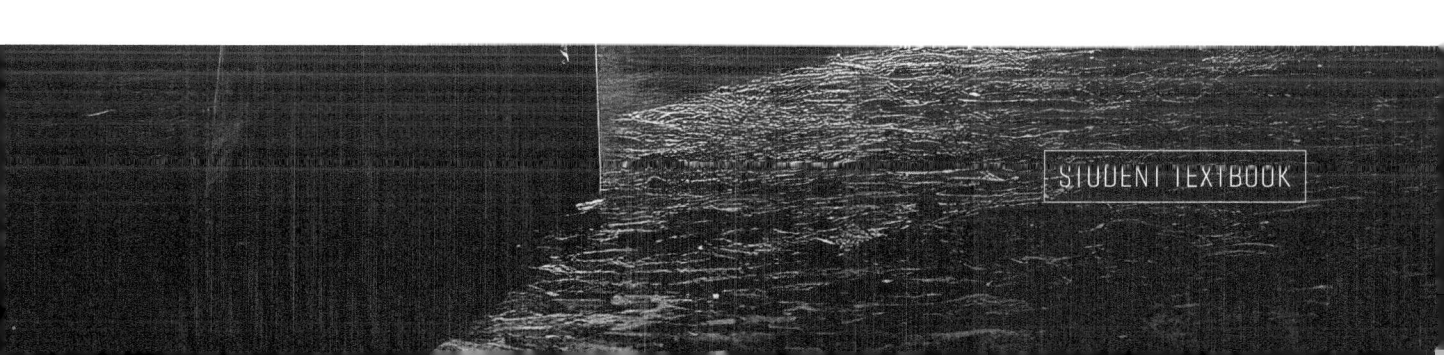

STUDENT TEXTBOOK

ADVISORY BOARD *of* GOVERNORS

Yaakov and Karen Cohen
Potomac, MD

Yitzchok and Julie Gniwisch
Montreal, QC

Barbara Hines
Aspen, CO

Ellen Marks
S. Diego, CA

David Mintz, OBM
Tenafly, NJ

George Rohr
New York, NY

Dr. Stephen F. Serbin
Columbia, SC

Leonard A. Wien, Jr.
Miami Beach, FL

PARTNERING FOUNDATIONS

Beinoni Foundation

David Samuel Rock Foundation

Diamond Foundation

Estate of Elliot James Belkin

Francine Gani Charitable Fund

Goldstein Family Foundation

The Harvey L. Miller Family Foundation

Kohelet Foundation

Kosins Family Foundation

Leticia and Eduardo Azar Foundation

Lion Heritage Fund at Rose Foundation

Meromim Foundation

Myra Reinhard Family Foundation

Robbins Family Foundation

Ruderman Family Foundation

Schulich Foundation

William Davidson Foundation

World Zionist Organization

Yehuda and Anne Neuberger Philanthropic Fund

Zalik Foundation

PRINCIPAL BENEFACTOR

George Rohr
New York, NY

PILLARS *of* JEWISH LITERACY

Shaya and Sarah Boymelgreen
Miami Beach, FL

Pablo and Sara Briman
Mexico City, Mexico

Zalman and Mimi Fellig
Miami Beach, FL

Edwin and Arlene Goldstein
Cincinnati, OH

Yosef and Chana Malka Gorowitz
Redondo Beach, CA

Shloimy and Mirele Greenwald
Brooklyn, NY

Dr. Vera Koch Groszmann
S. Paulo, Brazil

Carolyn Hessel
New York, NY

Edward and Inna Kholodenko
Toronto, ON

David and Debra Magerman
Gladwyne, PA

Yitzchak Mirilashvili
Herzliya, Israel

David and Harriet Moldau
Longwood, FL

Ben Nash
Sunny Isles Beach, FL

Eyal and Aviva Postelnik
Marietta, GA

Clive and Zoe Rock
Irvine, CA

Michael and Fiona Scharf
Palm Beach, FL

Lee and Patti Schear
Dayton, OH

Isadore and Roberta Schoen
Fairfax, VA

SPONSORS

Moshe and Rebecca Bolinsky
Long Beach, NY

Dr. Stephen and Bella Brenner
New York, NY

Rabbi Meyer and Leah Eichler
Brooklyn, NY

Steve and Esther Feder
Los Angeles, CA

Yoel Gabay
Brooklyn, NY

Dr. Gerald Gilbert Glass
Sunrise, FL

Shmuel and Sharone Goodman
Chicago, IL

Marc Kulick
New York, NY

Michael and Andrea Leven
Atlanta, GA

Joe and Shira Lipsey
Aspen, CO

Josef Michelashvili
Glendale, NY

Rachelle Nedow
El Paso, TX

Peter and Hazel Pflaum
Newport Beach, CA

Abraham Podolak
Princeton Junction, NJ

Dr. Ze'ev and Varda Rav-Noy
Los Angeles, CA

Arthur Isaac Resetschnig
Vienna, Austria

Zvi Ryzman
Los Angeles, CA

Larry Sifen
Virginia Beach, VA

Myrna Zisman
Cedarhurst, NY

Janice and Ivan Zuckerman
Coral Gables, FL

THE ROHR JEWISH LEARNING INSTITUTE
gratefully acknowledges the pioneering support of

George and Pamela Rohr

Since its inception, the JLI has been a beneficiary of the vision, generosity, care, and concern of the Rohr family.

In the merit of the tens of thousands of hours of Torah study by JLI students worldwide, may they be blessed with health, *Yiddishe nachas* from all their loved ones, and extraordinary success in all their endeavors.

DEDICATED TO

David and Harriet Moldau

Cherished partners with JLI in bringing the light of Torah to hundreds of communities around the world.

In the merit of the Torah studied worldwide, may they be blessed with good health, happiness, *nachas* from their loved ones, and success in all their endeavors.

IN TRIBUTE TO

Rabbi Moshe Kotlarsky

of blessed memory

הרב החסיד ר' משה יהודא ב"ר צבי יוסף ע"ה

Our longstanding visionary chairman, entrusted and empowered by the Rebbe to facilitate the growth and expansion of the network of Chabad shluchim and its institutions worldwide

יהא זכרו ברוך

Contents

1. **NOACH** 1
   RASHI: AN INTRODUCTION
   A Primer for a New Year of Torah Studies

2. **LECH LECHA** 19
   GLOBAL REACH, LOCAL CONCERN
   Never Too Big to Care for Those Closest to You

3. **VAYERA** 39
   A JEWISH TAKE ON HOSPITALITY
   Inviting Guests: Greater than Seeing G-d Himself

4. **CHAYEI SARAH** 55
   WHAT DO YOU LOVE ABOUT ISRAEL?
   IT'S MORE THAN FALAFEL AND THE IDF

5. **TOLDOS** 73
   IT'S NOT SO GOOD TO BE A GOODIE-GOODIE
   The Beauty of 'The Struggle'

6. **VAYETZEI** 87
   JACOB'S MORAL DILEMMA
   Don't Be Pious at Someone Else's Expense

7. **VAYISHLACH** 105
   BROADEN YOUR HORIZONS
   What an Ancient Sage's Travels Teach about Exploring New Ideas

8. **VAYESHEV** 119
   KEEP CLIMBING
   Trajectory Is All That Matters

9. **CHANUKAH** 135
   "TAKE THE FIRST STEP. I'LL DO THE REST."
   One Small Step from Man, One Giant Step from G-d

10. **VAYIGASH** 149
    WHEN YOU'RE IN PAIN, START YELLING
    Standing Up for Your Beliefs

11. **VAYECHI** 163
    YOU CAN CLEAN UP YOUR OWN MESS
    No Mistake Is Too Great to Fix

12. **SHEMOS** 179
    THE IDEAL JEW
    Hint: It's Not a Rabbi

1.
Noach

Rashi: An Introduction
A Primer for a New Year of Torah Studies

Dedicated in loving memory of Leah bas Shlomo Zev HaKohen Brenner,
מרת לאה בת שלמה זאב הכהן ע"ה,
marking her yahrtzeit on 24 Tishrei

May the merit of the Torah study worldwide accompany her soul in the world of everlasting life and be a source of blessings to her family with much health, happiness, nachas, and success.

PARSHAH OVERVIEW
Noach

G-d instructs Noah—the only righteous man in a world consumed by violence and corruption—to build a large wooden *tevah* ("ark"), coated within and without with pitch. A Great Deluge, says G-d, will wipe out all life from the face of the earth; but the ark will float upon the water, sheltering Noah and his family as well as two members (male and female) of each animal species.

Rain falls for forty days and nights, and the waters churn for 150 more days before calming and beginning to recede. The ark settles on Mount Ararat, and from its window Noah dispatches a raven, and then a series of doves, "to see if the waters were abated from the face of the earth." When the ground dries completely—exactly one solar year (365 days) after the onset of the Flood—G-d commands Noah to exit the *tevah* and repopulate the earth.

Noah builds an altar and offers sacrifices to G-d. G-d swears to never again destroy all of humankind because of their deeds, and He sets the rainbow as a testimony of His new covenant with the human race. G-d also commands Noah regarding the sacredness of life: murder is deemed a capital offense, and, while people are permitted to eat the meat of animals, they are forbidden to eat flesh or blood taken from a living animal.

Noah plants a vineyard and becomes drunk on its produce. Two of Noah's sons, Shem and Japheth, are blessed for covering up their father's nakedness, while his third son, Ham, is punished for taking advantage of his father's debasement.

INTRODUCTION

Rashi's Contemporaries

TEXT 1A

RABBI AVRAHAM IBN EZRA

> כּוֹכָב דָּרַךְ מִצָּרְפָתָה מַחֲנֵה עָרַךְ עַל יָטְבָתָה.
>
> ... פֵּרוּשׁ נוֹרָא שָׁם לַתּוֹרָה עַל כֵּן נִקְרָא פַּרְשָׁן דָּתָא.
>
> סִפְרוֹ גּוֹאֵל אֶל כָּל שׁוֹאֵל וּבְיִשְׂרָאֵל הוּא תִּרְצָתָה.

Rabbi Avraham ibn Ezra
1092–1167

Biblical commentator, linguist, and poet. Ibn Ezra was born in Toledo, Spain, and fled the Almohad regime to other parts of Europe. It is believed that he was living in London at the time of his death. Ibn Ezra is best known for his literalistic commentary on the Pentateuch. He also wrote works of poetry, philosophy, medicine, astronomy, and other topics.

A star has gone forth from France, a community established on firm foundations.

. . . An awe-inspiring commentary he penned, his sobriquet: exponent of faith.

His is a book of redemption for all who question, pleasing to the nation Israel.

TEXT 1B

NACHMANIDES, INTRODUCTION TO BIBLICAL COMMENTARY

> ואשים למאור פני נרות המנורה הטהורה, פרושי רבנו שלמה, עטרת צבי וצפירת תפארה.
>
> . . . לו משפט הבכורה, בדבריו אהגה, באהבתם אשגה.

I will place as illumination before me the lights of the pure candelabra, the commentaries of Rabbi Shlomo, a crown of glory, and a diadem of beauty. . . .

To him go the rights of the firstborn: I will study his words with soaring love.

Rabbi Moshe ben Nachman (Nachmanides, Ramban)
1194–1270

Scholar, philosopher, author, and physician. Nachmanides was born in Spain and served as leader of Iberian Jewry. In 1263, he was summoned by King James of Aragon to a public disputation with Pablo Cristiani, a Jewish apostate. Though Nachmanides was the clear victor of the debate, he had to flee Spain because of the resulting persecution. He moved to Israel and helped reestablish communal life in Jerusalem. He authored a classic commentary on the Pentateuch and a commentary on the Talmud.

TEXT 1C

RABBI MENACHEM ME'IRI, INTRODUCTION TO COMMENTARY ON MISHNAH, AVOT

> וראש לכל החיבורים שנתחברו דרך פירוש, הם פירושי רש"י זכרונו לברכה.
>
> ואם רבו הלוחמים עליו, כלי זיינו עליו ותשובתו מתוך דבריו כולם נכונים למבין.
>
> אין מעלתו נכרת רק ליחידים כי במילה אחת יכלול, לפעמים, תירוצים של חבילי קושיות.

Chief among all commentators is Rashi, of blessed memory.

If his attackers are numerous, he is equipped to defend, parrying with words succinct and wise.

Only select thinkers discern his greatness, deflecting bundles of questions with but a word.

Rabbi Menachem Me'iri
1249–1310

Talmudist and author. Me'iri was born in Provence, France. His monumental work, *Beit Habechirah*, summarizes in a lucid style the discussions of the Talmud along with the commentaries of the major subsequent rabbis. Despite its stature, the work was largely unknown for many generations, and thus has had less influence on subsequent Halachic development.

Rashi's Precision

TEXT 2A

RABBI YESHAYAHU HALEVI HOROWITZ, *SHENEI LUCHOT HABERIT, MASECHET SHEVU'OT* (OZ VEHADAR), P. 8

> כי חיבר החיבור שלו ברוח הקדש.

[Rashi] wrote his commentary with Divine inspiration.

Rabbi Yeshayahu Halevi Horowitz (*Shalah*)
1565–1630

Kabbalist and author. Rabbi Horowitz was born in Prague and served as rabbi in several prominent Jewish communities, including Frankfurt am Main and his native Prague. After the passing of his wife in 1620, he moved to Israel. In Tiberias, he completed his *Shenei Luchot Haberit*, an encyclopedic compilation of kabbalistic ideas. He is buried in Tiberias, next to Maimonides.

TEXT 2B

RABBI CHAIM YOSEF DAVID AZULAI, *SHEM HAGEDOLIM, MAARECHET SOFERIM, OT SHIN*

> ודקדק מאד בלשונו שרמז כמה חידושים בשינוי אות אחד.

He was extremely precise with his words, hinting at multiple teachings with the change of a single letter.

Rabbi Chaim Yosef David Azulai (*Chida*)
1724–1806

Talmudist and noted bibliophile. Born in Jerusalem, scion to a prominent rabbinic family, he studied under Rabbi Chaim ibn Atar. A prolific writer on various Jewish topics, his *Shem Hagedolim* is particularly famous, chronicling short biographies of Jewish authors with overviews of their works. He traveled extensively in Europe to raise funds on behalf of the Jewish community in the Land of Israel, and died in Italy.

I. THE PLAIN MEANING

Four Categories

TEXT 3A

ZOHAR, VOL. 3, RAYA MEHEMNA, P. 110A

בְּאוֹרַיְיתָא, פְּשָׁטִי"ם, רְאָיוֹ"ת, דְּרָשׁוֹ"ת, סוֹדוֹ"ת.
וּלְעֵילָא סִתְרֵי סְתָרִים לַה'.

Zohar

The seminal work of kabbalah, Jewish mysticism. The *Zohar* is a mystical commentary on the Torah, written in Aramaic and Hebrew. According to the Arizal, the *Zohar* contains the teachings of Rabbi Shimon bar Yocha'i, who lived in the Land of Israel during the 2nd century. The *Zohar* has become one of the indispensable texts of traditional Judaism, alongside and nearly equal in stature to the Mishnah and Talmud.

The Torah [can be understood on four levels]: the plain understanding, the allegorical understanding, the homiletical understanding, and the mystical understanding.

Beyond these are secrets upon secrets [known only] to G-d.

Rashi's Approach

TEXT 3B

RASHI, GENESIS 3:8

יֵשׁ מִדְרְשֵׁי אַגָּדָה רַבִּים וּכְבָר סִדְּרוּם רַבּוֹתֵינוּ עַל מְכוֹנָם בִּבְרֵאשִׁית רַבָּה וּבִשְׁאָר מִדְרָשׁוֹת.
וַאֲנִי לֹא בָּאתִי אֶלָּא לִפְשׁוּטוֹ שֶׁל מִקְרָא וּלְאַגָּדָה הַמְיַשֶּׁבֶת דִּבְרֵי הַמִּקְרָא דָּבָר דָּבוּר עַל אָפְנָיו.

Rabbi Shlomo Yitzchaki (Rashi)
1040–1105

Most noted biblical and Talmudic commentator. Born in Troyes, France, Rashi studied in the famed *yeshivot* of Mainz and Worms. His commentaries on the Pentateuch and the Talmud, which focus on the straightforward meaning of the text, appear in virtually every edition of the Talmud and Bible.

There are many Agadic [nonlegalistic explanations in the] Midrash. These were arranged by our sages in proper order in the Midrash, *Bereshit Rabah,* and other Midrashic texts.

I, however, have come only to teach the plain meaning of the text. And [I will also use] such Agadic texts that clarify the [plain meaning of the] biblical text, each word in its proper way.

TEXT 4

RABBI TUVIA BLAU, *KELALEI RASHI*, P. 15

> אנו מוצאים בעניין זה שיטות שונות אצל מפרשי רש"י.
>
> הרא"ם, למשל, סובר כי רש"י משתמש במדרש, "כל היכא דאיכא למידרש."
>
> לעומתו רבי דוד פראדו, אחד מגדולי פרשני רש"י, בספרו משכיל לדוד, כותב, "לא נחית רבינו לדרשה אלא אם כן הוכרח." כלומר כאשר הפשט אינו מספיק.
>
> לעומת אלה אנו מוצאים דעה שונה בתכלית, היא דעתו של בעל ספר זכרון, "מנהגו . . . שבוחר יותר במדרש . . . מהפשט הנראה לכאורה בישוב הכתוב." וביתר בהירות, "ברוב פסוקי התורה מניח פשט הכתוב ומביא מדרשם זכרונם לברכה. ואף על פי שלפעמים כותב, 'ואני ליישב פשוטו של מקרא באתי,' לאותו פסוק בלבד יכוון, לא לכל התורה."

Rabbi Tuvia Blau
1936–

Author and educator. A native of Jerusalem, Rabbi Tuvia Blau is the long-time principal of Beit Chana girls' high school in Jerusalem. A prominent Chabad activist and writer since the 1950s, he is known for his articles in journals and newspapers presenting the ideological positions of Chabad regarding current affairs. He is the author of *Kelalei Rashi*, summarizing the Lubavitcher Rebbe's innovative principles for the study of Rashi; and other works on Chabad thought and custom.

[With respect to this question] we find multiple approaches among the supercommentaries on Rashi.

Rabbi Eliyahu Mizrachi, for example, thought Rashi "makes use of homiletic interpretation wherever possible" [cited in the introduction to *Maskil LeDavid*].

In his [introduction to] *Maskil LeDavid*, Rabbi David Prado, one of the great supercommentators on Rashi, disagreed. He wrote, "Our teacher only made use of homily when absolutely necessary," meaning when the literal translation failed to satisfy.

On the other side of the spectrum, we find the opinion of [Rabbi Eliezer Ashkenazi, the] author of *Sefer Hazikaron*. [In his supercommentary to Exodus 13:17] he wrote that Rashi "chooses homiletic interpretation . . . over the obvious and plain meaning of the text." He stated even more clearly, "Rashi neglects the literal meaning of most biblical passages and relies instead on the homiletic interpretations of our sages, of blessed memory. When he wrote on several occasions 'I have only come to reconcile the plain meaning of the text,' he referred only to the specific passages under discussion, not to the entire Torah."

The Rebbe's Approach

TEXT 5

MISHNAH, AVOT 5:22

בֶּן חָמֵשׁ שָׁנִים לְמִקְרָא.

בֶּן עֶשֶׂר שָׁנִים לְמִשְׁנָה.

בֶּן שְׁלֹשׁ עֶשְׂרֵה לְמִצְוֹת.

בֶּן חֲמֵשׁ עֶשְׂרֵה לִגְמָרָא.

At the age of five, one studies Torah.

At the age of ten, one studies Mishnah.

At the age of thirteen, one is obligated in *mitzvot*.

At the age of fifteen, one studies the Talmud.

Avot
(Ethics of the Fathers; Pirkei Avot)

A 6-chapter work on Jewish ethics that is studied widely by Jewish communities, especially during the summer. The first 5 chapters are from the Mishnah, tractate Avot. Avot differs from the rest of the Mishnah in that it does not focus on legal subjects; it is a collection of the sages' wisdom on topics related to character development, ethics, healthy living, piety, and the study of Torah.

Rashi and the Child

TEXT 6A

THE REBBE, RABBI MENACHEM MENDEL SCHNEERSON,
TORAT MENACHEM 5744:2, P. 952

> כבר שקלו וטרו בקובצים בפירוש רש"י, ותירצו כמה תירוצים . . . אבל תירוצים אלו נכתבו באריכות גדולה, דף וחצי, וכיוצא בזה, ומתוך הבאת כמה וכמה מקורות מדברי חכמינו זכרונם לברכה, מפרשים, כו' עד למקור מלקוטי שיחות כרך פלוני, הערה פלונית.
>
> ומכיון שמדובר אודות בן חמש למקרא, טוען הוא מה רוצים ממנו עם אריכות גדולה כזו? רצונו להבין את דברי רש"י בפשטות ובקיצור כדי שיוכל אחר כך לשחק. ואין מה להסביר לו שקלא וטריא ארוכה עד להוכחה מ . . . כרך פלוני . . . הכתובה ללא נקודות.

Rabbi Menachem Mendel Schneerson
1902–1994

The towering Jewish leader of the 20th century, known as "the Lubavitcher Rebbe," or simply as "the Rebbe." Born in southern Ukraine, the Rebbe escaped Nazi-occupied Europe, arriving in the U.S. in June 1941. The Rebbe inspired and guided the revival of traditional Judaism after the European devastation, impacting virtually every Jewish community the world over. The Rebbe often emphasized that the performance of just one additional good deed could usher in the era of Mashiach. The Rebbe's scholarly talks and writings have been printed in more than 200 volumes.

The explanation for Rashi's comment was debated in several publications, and several answers were offered. . . . However, each answer took up, on average, a page and a half. They cited many teachings from our sages, of blessed memory, from other commentaries, even citing certain pages and footnotes from [my teachings in] *Likutei Sichot*.

However, we must remember that these explanations are presented to five-year-olds who wonder why we pester them with lengthy lectures. They want a simple and quick explanation of Rashi so they can go and play. Engaging in lengthy explanations with citations from Hebrew texts [especially texts] written without vowels, is off the mark.

TEXT 6B

THE REBBE, RABBI MENACHEM MENDEL SCHNEERSON,
SICHOT KODESH 5731:1, P. 243

> די אלע ענינים דארפן זיין מוכרח על פי פשטות הכתובים און רש"י דארף זיך ניט פארלאזן אויף דעם שפתי חכמים אדער אויף דעם מזרחי און די אנדערע פירושים. וואס זייער פירושים האט מען דאך געשריבען מיט הונדערטער יארען נאך רש"י. און בשעת רש"י האט דאס געלערנט מיט זיין תלמיד האט ער דאס פארשטאנען אן זייער פירושים.
>
> במילא דארף דאס אלץ זיין מוכרח על פי פשטות הכתובים.

Rashi [wrote his commentary in a manner that his] teachings are obvious from a plain reading of the biblical text. Rashi does not rely on the supercommentaries of *Siftei Chachamim*, Rabbi Mizrachi, or others to explain his meaning. These commentaries were written hundreds of years after Rashi wrote his commentary. When Rashi taught his students, they understood him without the aid of these commentaries.

Therefore we, too, should be able to understand Rashi by perusing the plain meaning of the biblical text.

TEXT 7

THE REBBE, RABBI MENACHEM MENDEL SCHNEERSON, IBID., PP. 138–139

> די מפרשים אויף פירוש רש"י זיינען בעיקר מפרש רש"י על דרך ההלכה, על דרך הרמז, על דרך הדרוש, און על דרך הסוד. וואס בנוגע דרך הסוד איז דאס בעיקר דער פירוש פון מהר"ל מפראג, גור אריה, וואס בכמה מקומות לערנט ער רש"י על דרך הסוד שבתורה.

The supercommentaries on Rashi primarily explain Rashi in the manner of Halachah, allegory, homily, or mysticism. With respect to the latter, it is primarily the commentary of Rabbi Yehudah Leib Loew from Prague, author of *Gur Aryeh*, who often explained Rashi according to the mystical tradition.

LESSON 1 / RASHI: AN INTRODUCTION

II. INTRODUCING THE RASHI *SICHAH*

The Rashi Sichah

TEXT 8

"REVOLUTION IN RASHI," *A CHASSIDISHE DERHER*, 28 SHEVAT 5775, P. 42

The Rebbe arrived at his place. Instead of starting his *sichah* as soon as he sat down, as he usually did, the Rebbe requested that a *Chumash* [a copy of the Pentateuch] be brought to him. That the Rebbe should request a book during a *farbrengen* was extremely rare. It was the first indication that something unusual was underway.

The *Chumash* was brought, and . . . the Rebbe opened it to *parshat Noach*, and began reading and translating the first passage. He then moved on to Rashi, reading and translating the second Rashi on the *parshah*.

It was a beautiful scene; hundreds of Chasidim crowding around as the Rebbe sat and taught Rashi like a teacher in *cheder*. First translating, and then proceeding to ask several penetrating questions, cutting to the very heart of Rashi's words.

No one realized it at the time, but this was a historic moment. The Rebbe had just—quietly and without much fanfare—launched a revolution that would accompany every Shabbat *farbrengen* for the next 23 years and would change the way we look at Rashi.

A Unified Approach

TEXT 9

THE REBBE, RABBI MENACHEM MENDEL SCHNEERSON, *LIKUTEI SICHOT* 29, P. 213

> ווי גערעט כמה פעמים איז תורתינו הקדושה א תורה אחת. פנימיות התורה און חלק ההלכה שבתורה זיינען כולא חד . . . ווי א גוף ונשמה.
>
> דאס הייסט אז אלע חלקי התורה זיינען מחאים מיט די אנדערע און זיינען עולה בקנה אחד.

I have explained many times that our holy Torah is a single Torah. The inner dimension of the Torah and the Halachic dimension of the Torah are all one, . . . like a body and soul.

This means that all the sections of the Torah fit together like multiple parts of a single branch.

The Rashi Wonders

TEXT 10A

RABBI YESHAYAHU HALEVI HOROWITZ, *SHENEI LUCHOT HABERIT, MASECHET SHEVU'OT* (OZ VEHADAR), P. 8

> כי בכל דיבור ודיבור של רש"י יש דברים נסתרים נפלאים . . . צאו וראו ברש"י שעל התורה, שהקורא סובר שהוא קל, ראו . . . ותמצאו נפלאות.

There are hidden wondrous teachings in every word of Rashi. . . . Peruse Rashi's comments on the Torah. At face value, you might think it is light reading, but look, . . . and you will find *wonders*.

The Rashi Wine

TEXT 10B

HAYOM YOM, 29 SHEVAT

> דער אלטער רבי האט אמאל געזאגט: פירוש רש״י אויף חומש איז
> יינה של תורה, פותח הלב ומגלה אהבה ויראה עצמיות.

Rabbi Shneur Zalman of Liadi, [also known as] the Alter Rebbe, once said, "Rashi's commentary on the Torah is the wine of the Torah. It opens the heart, bringing to the surface our inherent love and awe of G-d."

Hayom Yom

In 1942, Rabbi Yosef Yitzchak Schneersohn, the 6th rebbe of Chabad, gave his son-in-law, the future Rebbe, the task of compiling an anthology of Chasidic aphorisms and customs arranged according to the days of the year. In describing the completed product, Rabbi Yosef Yitzchak wrote that it is "a book that is small in format but bursting with pearls and diamonds of the choicest quality."

TEXT 10C

RABBI MORDECHAI YOFFE, *LEVUSHEI OR YEKAROS* (LUBLIN, 1595), P. 23

> כל הדברים שבפירוש רש״י יש בהם נגלה ונסתר. ושניהם אמת.

Every word in Rashi's commentary contains a revealed understanding and concealed strata. Both are true.

Rabbi Mordechai Yoffe
1530–1612

Student of Rabbi Moshe Isserlis; served as rabbi in Prague, Lublin, Hurdna, and Posen. He was one of the leaders of the Council of Four Lands, a central body of Jewish authority in Poland. He authored the *Levush*, a code of law that is more comprehensive than the concise style of the Shulchan Aruch.

TEXT 10D

THE REBBE, RABBI MENACHEM MENDEL SCHNEERSON, *LIKUTEI SICHOT* 5, P. 1

> דער פירוש פון רש״י על התורה, הגם אז ער קומט צו מפרש זיין
> פשוטו של מקרא . . . אנטהאלט ער אבער אויך ענינים מופלאים
> פון די אנדערע חלקי התורה, אפילו אויך רזין דאורייתא. וכידוע דער
> ווארט פון אלטן רבין אז "פירוש רש״י אויף חומש איז יינה של תורה."
>
> נאר בכדי צו קענען דערגרונטעווען זיך צו די ענינים מופלאים און
> יינה של תורה וואס אין פירוש רש״י מוז מען פריער דורכלערנען און
> פארשטיין דעם פירוש הפשוט. ווייל אויך זיי, די ענינים מופלאים
> און יינה של תורה האט רש״י אריינגעשטעלט אין דעם פירוש לויט
> פשוטו של מקרא.

Although Rashi's commentary on the Torah explains the plain meaning of the text, it also contains wondrous teachings from other sections of the Torah, including the mystical mysteries of the Torah. As Rabbi Shneur Zalman of Liadi, the Alter Rebbe, famously said, "Rashi's commentary on the Torah is the wine of the Torah."

However, to dig through to the wondrous teachings and the wine of the Torah, we must first study the plain meaning of Rashi's commentary. Because Rashi embedded the wondrous teachings and the wine of the Torah *into* the plain meaning of the Torah's text.

LESSON 1 / RASHI: AN INTRODUCTION

KEY POINTS

- » Rashi's commentary on the Torah explains the plain meaning of the biblical text.

- » Rashi's commentary was revered by his contemporaries and ever since. More than three hundred supercommentaries were written on Rashi.

- » They outline the questions that Rashi addressed and explain his often enigmatic language.

- » The Rebbe presented an original way to analyze Rashi that demonstrates Rashi's commitment to the plain meaning of the text. At the same time, the Rebbe extracted many deep nuggets from Rashi's commentary.

- » In the course of his teachings, the Rebbe articulated hundreds of hermeneutic principles by which Rashi operated when writing his commentary.

APPENDIX

TEXT 11

RABBI TUVIA BLAU, *KELALEI RASHI*, PP. 71–112

ענינו של רש"י הוא לפרש את הכתובים אך ורק לפי פשוטם...ואפילו אם הדברים סותרים את כל הדעות...בדרך ההלכה....משמעות המושג פשט היא בדרגתו הפשוטה ביותר...שהדברים יובנו אפילו על ידי ילד בן חמש.

הוא בא לסלק ולתרץ כל קושי...העלול להתעורר בהתאם לרמת ידיעותיו של בן חמש. כיוון שכן כאשר יש קושי ש...ברור מאיליו ההסבר לבן החמש...אין רש"י טורח להסביר אותו.

בדרך כלל הוא מתחיל מיד בהסברת הענין באופן שהקושי מסולק אגב הרצאת הדברים...עלינו לבדוק היטב איזה קושי בא רש"י לסלק.

מאחר ובן החמש לומד את התורה לפי סדר, סומך רש"י בכל מקום בתורה על דברים האמורים בתורה לפני כן.

רש"י מביא שני פירושים לדבר אחד כאשר יש קושי לפי הפשט בכל אחד בהם והם משלימים זה את זה...הפירוש הראשון הוא העקרי משום שהוא חלק יותר וקרוב יותר לפשוטו של מקרא.

רוב מאמרי חכמינו זכרונם לברכה המצוטטים בפירוש רש"י באים ללא ציון מקורם ומבלי להגדירם כמדרשיים. במקרים אלה הדרשות מתחייבים בהכרח מפשוטו של מקרא.

ביטויים כמו "דרשו רבותינו" "מדרש" באו לאמר שאין פירוש זה חלק לגמרי...אם כי הוא יכול להתאים לפשוטו של מקרא.

רש"י מצטט בדבור המתחיל רק את המלים אותן הוא בא לבאר...ולא יותר...ולא פחות...כן מעתיק רש"י את המלים שמהן הכרח לפירושו.

ברוב המקרים אין הוא מציין את מקורם שכן ציון המקור אינו הכרחי להבנת פשוטו של מקרא. כאשר רש"י מציין מקור לדבריו, מהווה רמז למקרה שאצל התלמיד יתעורר קושי מסויים...שאז תמצא התשובה במקור המסומן.

LESSON 1 / RASHI: AN INTRODUCTION

Rashi's purpose is to explain the plain meaning of the text, . . . even if this contradicts all the Halachic opinions. . . . When we say plain, we refer to the plainest meaning, . . . one that is understood by a five-year-old.

Rashi's purpose is to address every difficulty that might arise on the level of a five-year-old's knowledge. Therefore, when the answer is obvious to the child, Rashi doesn't bother to explain it.

Rashi typically begins by immediately presenting the explanation such that all questions fall away. . . . It's the student's job to determine which questions Rashi was looking to address.

Inasmuch as the five-year-old studies the Torah in order, Rashi relied in all cases on what the Torah [and Rashi] explained earlier.

Rashi brings two explanations when each is not perfectly consistent with the plain meaning of the text and when each complements the other. . . . [In such cases] the first explanation that Rashi offers is primary because it is smoother and closer to the plain meaning of the text.

In most instances, Rashi quotes our sages without citing the source and without identifying them as a Midrash. In these instances, the Midrash is consistent with the plain meaning of the text.

When Rashi uses phrases such as "our sages taught" or "Midrash," he intends to inform us that this explanation is not entirely consistent with the text's plain meaning, . . . though it can be made to fit it.

Rashi only cites the words from the passage that he intends to address. . . . He never cites an additional word. . . . He never fails to cite a word that he addresses. . . . Rashi also cites words from the passage that serve as proof for his explanation.

In most instances, Rashi does not cite the source of a teaching because the source doesn't aid our understanding of the plain meaning of the text. When Rashi does cite the source, it indicates that a question might arise. In this case, the answer can be found by examining the original source text.

2.
Lech Lecha

Global Reach, Local Concern
Never Too Big to Care for Those Closest to You

*Dedicated to Yael Roth in appreciation for her friendship
and partnership with JLI and her dedication to bringing
the light of Torah to communities across the globe*

PARSHAH OVERVIEW

Lech Lecha

G-d speaks to Abram, commanding him, "Go from your land, from your birthplace, and from your father's house, to the land that I will show you." There, G-d says, he will be made into a great nation. Abram and his wife, Sarai, accompanied by his nephew Lot, journey to the land of Canaan, where Abram builds an altar and continues to spread the message of a single G-d.

A famine forces the first Jew to depart for Egypt, where beautiful Sarai is taken to Pharaoh's palace; Abram escapes death because they present themselves as brother and sister. A plague prevents the Egyptian king from touching her and convinces him to return her to Abram and to compensate the brother-revealed-as-husband with gold, silver, and cattle.

Back in the land of Canaan, Lot separates from Abram and settles in the evil city of Sodom, where he falls captive when the mighty armies of Chedorla'omer and his three allies conquer the five cities of the Sodom Valley. Abram sets out with a small band to rescue his nephew, defeats the four kings, and is blessed by Melchizedek, the king of Salem (Jerusalem).

G-d seals the Covenant between the Parts with Abram, in which the exile and persecution (*Galut*) of the people of Israel is foretold, and the Holy Land is bequeathed to them as their eternal heritage.

Still childless ten years after their arrival in the Land, Sarai tells Abram to marry her maidservant Hagar. Hagar conceives, becomes insolent toward her mistress, and then flees when Sarai treats her harshly; an angel convinces her to return and tells her that her son will father a populous nation. Ishmael is born in Abram's eighty-sixth year.

Thirteen years later, G-d changes Abram's name to Abraham ("father of multitudes") and Sarai's to Sarah ("princess") and promises that a son will be born to them; from this child, whom they are to call Isaac ("will laugh"), will stem the great nation with which G-d will establish His special bond. Abraham is commanded to circumcise himself and his descendants as a "sign of the covenant between Me and you." Abraham immediately complies, circumcising himself and all the males of his household.

INTRODUCTION

Question for Discussion

What advice would you give someone who asks you how to set priorities and balance competing responsibilities?

Here are the exegetical rules we will use to examine this Rashi.

1. Rashi only attributes meaning to a name when the text requires it.
2. If a word requires an explanation, Rashi explains it the first time it appears.
3. Rashi does not use unusual phrases unless they add to our understanding.

I. A NAME CHANGE

TEXT 1A

GENESIS 17:5

> וְלֹא יִקָּרֵא עוֹד אֶת שִׁמְךָ אַבְרָם, וְהָיָה שִׁמְךָ אַבְרָהָם כִּי אַב הֲמוֹן גּוֹיִם נְתַתִּיךָ.

Your name will no longer be called Abram; your name will be Abraham because I appointed you father to multitudes of nations.

TEXT 1B

RASHI, AD LOC.

> "כִּי אַב הֲמוֹן גּוֹיִם":
>
> לְשׁוֹן נוֹטָרִיקוֹן שֶׁל שְׁמוֹ.
>
> וְרֵי"שׁ שֶׁהָיְתָה בּוֹ בַּתְּחִלָּה - שֶׁלֹּא הָיָה אָב אֶלָּא לַאֲרָם שֶׁהוּא מְקוֹמוֹ, וְעַכְשָׁו אָב לְכָל הָעוֹלָם - לֹא זָזָה מִמְּקוֹמָהּ.

"Because I appointed you father to multitudes of nations":

[Abraham is] an acrostic for *av hamon goyim* [Hebrew for "father of the multitude of nations"].

The letter *resh*, which was in his original name, connoted that he was father only to the nation of Aram—his native land. [Though] he was now father to the entire world, this letter did not move from its place.

Rabbi Shlomo Yitzchaki (Rashi)
1040–1105

Most noted biblical and Talmudic commentator. Born in Troyes, France, Rashi studied in the famed *yeshivot* of Mainz and Worms. His commentaries on the Pentateuch and the Talmud, which focus on the straightforward meaning of the text, appear in virtually every edition of the Talmud and Bible.

II. THE STUBBORN LETTER

Unwitting Prophecy

TEXT 2

RABBI CHAIM VITAL, *SHAAR HAGILGULIM,* CH. 23

> כאשר נולד האדם, וקוראים לו אביו ואמו שם אחד העולה בדעתם, אינו באקראי ובהזדמן, כי אם הקדוש ברוך הוא משים בפיו השם ההוא המוכרח אל הנשמה ההיא.

When a child is born and the parents choose a name, the name choice is not random. G-d places the name that belongs to their child's soul in the parents' minds.

Rabbi Chaim Vital
c. 1542–1620

Lurianic kabbalist. Rabbi Vital was born in Israel, lived in Safed and Jerusalem, and later lived in Damascus. He was authorized by his teacher, Rabbi Yitzchak Luria, the Arizal, to record his teachings. Acting on this mandate, Vital began arranging his master's teachings in written form, and his many works constitute the foundation of the Lurianic school of Jewish mysticism. His most famous work is *Etz Chayim*.

The Out-of-Place Letter

TEXT 3A

THE REBBE, RABBI MENACHEM MENDEL SCHNEERSON, *LIKUTEI SICHOT* 25, P. 65

> און דאס דייטעט אן רש"י בלשונו - "ואפילו רי"ש שהיתה בו בתחלה, שלא היה אב אלא לארם שהוא מקומו כו'".
>
> דערמיט זאגט רש"י אז דא איז דא א קשיא: לויט נוטריקון, ווי קומט דער רי"ש אין שם אברהם?
>
> ובמילא - מוז אויך דער רי"ש האבן א פירוש בהתאם צום תוכן השם אברהם - "אב המון גוים".

This is what Rashi means when he writes, "The letter *resh*, which was in his original name, connoted that he was father only to the nation of Aram—his native land."

With these words, Rashi informs us that there is a problem: the letter *resh* does not belong in the Abraham acrostic.

Its presence in the new acrostic tells us that the name Abram also has meaning: A meaning that is consistent with the meaning of Abraham—father of multitudes of nations.

**Rabbi Menachem Mendel Schneerson
1902–1994**

The towering Jewish leader of the 20th century, known as "the Lubavitcher Rebbe," or simply as "the Rebbe." Born in southern Ukraine, the Rebbe escaped Nazi-occupied Europe, arriving in the U.S. in June 1941. The Rebbe inspired and guided the revival of traditional Judaism after the European devastation, impacting virtually every Jewish community the world over. The Rebbe often emphasized that the performance of just one additional good deed could usher in the era of Mashiach. The Rebbe's scholarly talks and writings have been printed in more than 200 volumes.

What Does Abram Mean?

TEXT 3B

THE REBBE, RABBI MENACHEM MENDEL SCHNEERSON, IBID.

> און רש"י איז מבאר "שלא היה אב אלא לארם כו' לא זזה מקומה".
>
> דער תוכן פון דעם רש"י איז - וואס ער איז "אב לארם", און דער ענין איז דאך געבליבן אויך דערנאך.
>
> "אב לכל הגוים" איז כולל, און ניט שולל דעם ענין פון "אב לארם", עס איז נאר א הוספה.

Rashi goes on to explain the meaning of Abram: "He was only the father of Aram . . . [and] this did not move from its place."

With this, Rashi informs us that the letter *resh* [of the original name] means that he is the father of Aram. And this [kinship to Aram] remained in place after the name change.

[In other words, the new name] father to all nations, did not exclude fatherhood to Aram. It includes Aram and expands on it [to include all the nations].

Abraham Never Budged

TEXT 3C

THE REBBE, RABBI MENACHEM MENDEL SCHNEERSON, IBID.

> און דאס איז דיוק לשון רש"י - "לא זזה ממקומה" (און זאגט ניט "לא נטלה ממנו" כו' כנזכר לעיל).
>
> אפילו ווען מען וואלט דעם רי"ש ניט אריינגעשטעלט בשמו (און שמו וואלט געווען "אבהם") וואלט עס ניט געמיינט אז מ'האט צוגענומען דעם תוכן פון דעם רי"ש - זיין תוכן ("אב לארם") בלייבט אויך דעמאלט. אבער אין דעם פאל וואלט עס באדייט אז דער רי"ש "בלייבט" אין א צווייטן "מקום" - נאר אלס טייל פון "עולם" – "אב לכל העולם".
>
> די הדגשה אין "לא זזה ממקומה" טוט אויף אז אויך דערנאך בלייבט דער רי"ש אין זיין "מקום", דער "אב לארם" בלייבט מפורט בנוטריקון אינעם שם (אברהם) אלס אן ענין פאר זיך (אף על פי וואס ער איז בכלל פון "(אב ל)כל העולם").

This is why Rashi used the phrase "did not move from its place" rather than "was not removed from it" or the like.

Even if the letter *resh* were erased from the new name, rendering the new name Abham, it would not imply the cancelation of its meaning. Abraham's role as father to Aram would have remained intact. However, it would have implied that the *resh* [Abraham's relationship with Aram] had been folded into Abraham's new status as father to the world.

By saying that "it did not leave its place," Rashi emphasizes that the *resh* remained rooted in place. Abraham's role as father to Aram stood out in the new acrostic because his role as father to Aram remained independently significant despite his new role as father to the world.

LESSON 2 / GLOBAL REACH, LOCAL CONCERN

III. WHAT'S IN A NAME?

Do Names Have Meaning?

TEXT 4A

RABBI AVRAHAM IBN EZRA, GENESIS 10:8

> אל תבקש טעם לכל השמות אם לא נכתב.

Don't seek meaning for names to which the Torah does not attribute meaning.

Rabbi Avraham ibn Ezra
1092–1167

Biblical commentator, linguist, and poet. Ibn Ezra was born in Toledo, Spain, and fled the Almohad regime to other parts of Europe. It is believed that he was living in London at the time of his death. Ibn Ezra is best known for his literalistic commentary on the Pentateuch. He also wrote works of poetry, philosophy, medicine, astronomy, and other topics.

TEXT 4B

NACHMANIDES, GENESIS 23:9

> ואין צורך לבקש טעם לשם המקומות.

There is no need to seek meanings for the names of places.

Rabbi Moshe ben Nachman
(Nachmanides, Ramban)
1194–1270

Scholar, philosopher, author, and physician. Nachmanides was born in Spain and served as leader of Iberian Jewry. In 1263, he was summoned by King James of Aragon to a public disputation with Pablo Cristiani, a Jewish apostate. Though Nachmanides was the clear victor of the debate, he had to flee Spain because of the resulting persecution. He moved to Israel and helped reestablish communal life in Jerusalem. He authored a classic commentary on the Pentateuch and a commentary on the Talmud.

IV. TRUE TO YOUR ROOTS

Three Tiers

TEXT 5

THE REBBE, RABBI MENACHEM MENDEL SCHNEERSON,
IGROT MELECH 2, PP. 292–294

> בחיי אנוש עלי אדמות, והרי העיקר אצל האדם הוא חייו הרוחניים, חלוקים באופן כללי לשלושה תחומים, ובכל אחד מהם נדרשת הדרגה הגבוהה ביותר של שלימות שאליה מסוגל כל אחד להגיע . . .
>
> שלושת התחומים הם:
>
> ראשית, להגיע לשלימות עצמית המקיפה את האדם בשלימותו ואת כל הנהגתו . . .
>
> התחום השני בחיי האדם הוא הקשר שלו עם אנשים אחרים ועם כל הסביבה. לעשות ולפעול בעזרה וסיוע לאנשים שאתם הוא בא במגע, להביא שלימות בחייהם ובכלל להכניס אלקות וקדושה.
>
> התחום השלישי בחיי האדם קשור באותו חלק מן העולם אשר לכאורה אין לו שייכות אליו. הוא רחוק ממנו בפשטות, או מבחינה רוחנית, והוא לא מסוגל להגיע אליו. ברם חייב אדם לומר, "בשבילי נברא העולם" (סנהדרין ד, ה). הכרחי איפוא, למצוא דרך להשפיע גם על חלק זה.

Our primary responsibility in life is to make ourselves spiritually whole. This can be divided into three general tiers, and we must do our best in each. . . .

The three tiers are:

First is to be the best that we can be in terms of character and behavior. . . .

The second is our relationship with our community. To assist everyone, we strive to be the best that we can be and introduce G-dliness and holiness to our surroundings.

The third is a tier for which we are ostensibly not responsible. These are people beyond our physical or spiritual reach. However, we must do our best to reach them, too, for one is obligated to say, "The world was created for me [to improve]" (Sanhedrin 4:5). Therefore, they, too, are within our scope of responsibility.

Begin with Yourself

TEXT 6

THE REBBE, RABBI MENACHEM MENDEL SCHNEERSON,
TORAT MENACHEM 5743:4, P. 1743

> אף שתפקידו של האדם הוא להתייגע ולנצל את כחותיו כדי לפעול בכל הסביבה כולה, ועד לפעולה והשפעה בכל העולם כולו - הרי כדי שעבודה זו תהיה עבודה מסודרת, עליו להתחיל - לכל לראש - עם עצמו . . . כלומר, לכל לראש עליו לדעת בעצמו את המעשה אשר יעשה כו', להתנהג על פי צדק ויושר.
>
> ומהפרט מגיע הוא אל הכלל, היינו, כאשר הנהגתו האישית תהיה כדבעי, אזי יוכל להפעיל את השפעתו בסביבתו. לכל לראש בשכונתו, ואחר כך בעירו וכו', עד להשפעה בחוגי המלוכה. וכל זה - כאמור - לאחרי הוראת "דוגמא חיה" מהנהגתו האישית.
>
> ונוסף לזה, רק כאשר הנהגתו האישית היא באופן המתאים, זוכה הוא לברכתו של הקדוש ברוך הוא שיצליח בהשפעתו על הסביבה כולה. וכפי שרואים בפועל - "מעשה רב" - שההצלחה בעסקנות ציבורית (באיזה שטח שתהיה) תלויה במדה רבה ומכרעת באופן הנהגתו האישית. היינו, שכאשר הנהגתו האישית היא כדבעי, אזי גדולה השפעתו על כל אלו שנמצאים מסביבו, מפני שהם מעריכים, מוקירים, ומכבדים אותו על הנהגתו האישית על פי צדק ויושר.

Though it is our mission to utilize our talents and abilities to impact our surroundings and the entire world, it must begin with us.

. . . First, we must ensure that our own behavior is just and appropriate, and only then can we influence others. Once we ensure the propriety of our behavior, we can exert positive influence on others. First others in our neighborhoods, then in our city, etc., until our influence extends to government officials and national leaders. It all begins with being a living example in our personal lives.

Moreover, only when our personal behavior is fitting can we merit Divine blessing to influence others successfully. We see this from experience. The success of any community activist depends largely on the activist's personal integrity. When we behave appropriately, our circle of influence expands because people value, esteem, and respect our propriety and integrity.

TEXT 7

MAGGIE ETHRIDGE, "PROTEST V PARENTHOOD: HOW THE CHILDREN OF POLITICAL ACTIVISTS SUFFER IN SILENCE," WWW.THEGUARDIAN.COM

Rebecca Walker is a case in point. . . . Walker has long struggled to come to terms with how her parents' civil rights activism absorbed her childhood. . . .

"My parents were so deeply involved in the civil rights movement that a lot of my needs as a young person were not fully seen and addressed, or considered as important as the movement. . . . It wasn't an intentional neglect. . . . [They were] missing what was happening in our lives because there was so much consuming their lives. It felt very lonely and vulnerable. Gandhi's children had a lot of problems with him; it's hard to find children of very visible and profound activists whose children felt cared for and nurtured in the same way the movements were." . . .

The words "anxiety," "insecurity," and "no communication" come up frequently in interviews of children of rigorous activists—something meticulously documented in John Blake's book, *The Children of the Movement*, which catalogs a series of interviews with the adult children of civil rights activist leaders. Most expressed a lifelong anxiety about their relevance in their own families, but also about whether they had even been seen as a person outside of the concerns of the movement.

In many cases, consent was not even considered; devotion was required. As Brown writes, "A large number of [adult children of activists] are emotionally distant from their parents who, they say, are more suited for protest than parenthood."

TEXT 8

RABBI MOSHE MILLER, *THE NECHOMAH GREIZMAN ANTHOLOGY*, SECTION TWO, FAMILY HARMONY

While you are working with your hands, talk to them and listen to them. Try to do work that requires concentration when they're not around, and easier work when they are.

Look for small opportunities to spend time alone with each child—even if only for a few minutes. One excellent method is to take only one child with you in a rotation system when you go out to the dentist, shopping, bank, etc. It makes the child feel very special. Buy him a little treat and talk to him, and the rewards will come.

Our Community

TEXT 9

MAIMONIDES, *MISHNEH TORAH*, LAWS OF GIFTS TO THE POOR 7:13

> עָנִי שֶׁהוּא קְרוֹבוֹ, קֹדֶם לְכָל אָדָם.
>
> עֲנִיֵּי בֵּיתוֹ, קוֹדְמִין לַעֲנִיֵּי עִירוֹ.
>
> עֲנִיֵּי עִירוֹ, קוֹדְמִין לַעֲנִיֵּי עִיר אַחֶרֶת.
>
> שֶׁנֶּאֱמַר: "לְאָחִיךָ, לַעֲנִיֶּךָ, וּלְאֶבְיֹנְךָ בְּאַרְצֶךָ" (דְּבָרִים טו, יא).

A poor person in your family comes first.

Poor people in your household receive priority over poor people in the city.

Poor people in your city receive priority over poor people in other cities.

This is inferred from [the order of] the passage, "To your brother, to your poor person, and to the needy in your land" (Deuteronomy 15:11).

Rabbi Moshe ben Maimon (Maimonides, Rambam) 1135–1204

Halachist, philosopher, author, and physician. Maimonides was born in Córdoba, Spain. After the conquest of Córdoba by the Almohads, he fled Spain and eventually settled in Cairo, Egypt. There, he became the leader of the Jewish community and served as court physician to the vizier of Egypt. He is most noted for authoring the *Mishneh Torah*, an encyclopedic arrangement of Jewish law; and for his philosophical work, *Guide for the Perplexed*. His rulings on Jewish law are integral to the formation of Halachic consensus.

TEXT 10

THE REBBE, RABBI MENACHEM MENDEL SCHNEERSON, *IGROT KODESH* 29, PP. 249–250

> וביחד עם זה תמהתי תמיה רבה שכאילו היתה הצעה שכבוד תורתו
> יחשוב ויתענין להעתיק מעירו למדינה אחרת וכו'. ואף שבטוחני
> שאין זה מעשיי כלל וכלל, שהרי רבים צריכים לכבוד תורתו, ולא רק
> בעירו האמורה ממש, אשר גם היא עיר ואם כו', אלא גם בסביבותיה,
> ובכל המדינה ובמדינות הסמוכות, וצריכים להוראת במעשה בפועל
> ולהתעוררות בעבודת ה' באהבת ה' וביראת ה' וכו' וכו'.
>
> בכל זה מרשה אני לעצמי להעלות על הכתב את הכתוב לעיל בגודל
> הבטחון - שבודאי ובודאי ימשיך לנהל קהילא קדישא דיליה והמדינה
> כולה בהיותו במקומו עתה. ויאריך ימים על ממלכתו (מאן מלכי רבנן),
> ומתוך נחת שדבריו מתקבלים והנהגתו מצליחה.
>
> ואם הוראת חכמינו זכרונם לברכה היא "עניי עירך קודמים", על אחת
> כמה וכמה עניי מדינה כולה קודמים. ולדכותיה דכבוד תורתו האריכות
> בהאמור אך למותר. ובטוחני שכיוונתי לדעת כבוד תורתו בלאו הכי,
> ובסגנון הידוע "מקומך אל תנח" (קהלת י, ד). ואדרבה - יוסיף חיל לחזק
> שם לימוד דבר ה', ותורתו והידור קיום מצוותיו, במרוקו וסביבותיה וכו',
> וזכות הרבים מסייעת.

I was surprised to hear that your honor was advised to consider relocating to a different country. I am certain the suggestion is impractical considering the multitudes, not only in your city—itself a thriving community—but also in its environs, in the country at large, and in neighboring countries, who require your honor's mentorship. They require your Halachic guidance and your inspiration to love and fear G-d, etc.

Nevertheless, I permit myself to write about this in the confidence that you will certainly continue to lead your sacred congregation and the country in which you reside. May you continue in your seat of rabbinic governance for many years, and may you experience the joy of witnessing the efficacy of your work.

LESSON 2 / GLOBAL REACH, LOCAL CONCERN

If our sages of blessed memory taught, "The poor people of your city come first" (*Mishneh Torah,* Laws of Gifts to the Poor 7:13), it is certainly true that the poor people of your entire country come first. For one such as yourself, elaboration is quite superfluous. I am certain that you are of similar mind in accordance with the well-known saying, "Do not abandon your place" (Ecclesiastes 10:4).

May you continue to strengthen Torah study and observance in Morocco and its environs, and may the merit of the entire community stand by you.

TEXT 11

THE REBBE, RABBI MENACHEM MENDEL SCHNEERSON, *LIKUTEI SICHOT* 25, P. 69

> אף על פי אז א איד דארף אויפטאן בכל העולם כולו, דארף ער אבער וויסן, אז לכל לראש ליגט אויף אים א חיוב צו משפיע זיין על מקומו וסביבתו, און ערשט דערנאך, ווען ער ווערט אן "אב למקומו", צו זיין אן "אב לכל העולם".

Though all Jews must exert whatever influence they can the world over, they must know that their first obligation is to their local community. Only after becoming a "father" to your local community can you become a "father" to the world at large.

KEY POINTS

» Abraham's first life mission was to be the spiritual father of Aram, his birthplace. His father unwittingly called him Abram, an acronym for *av aram*—father of Aram.

» When he was ninety-nine, G-d appointed him father to all nations. At that time, G-d changed his name to Abraham, an acronym of *av hamon*—father to multitudes.

» A proper acrostic would be Abham. G-d called him Abraham to indicate that though his portfolio expanded, his first responsibility to Aram remained intact.

» From this we learn that though we must help every person we can reach, our first responsibility is to those who are closest to us.

» Our pyramid of responsibilities is three tiered. First ourselves and our children. Then our local community. Finally, people from afar. We must help everyone, but those closest to us come first.

3.
Vayera

A Jewish Take on Hospitality
Inviting Guests: Greater than Seeing G-d Himself

Dedicated in loving memory of Mrs. Charlotte Rohr,
מרת שרה ע"ה בת ר' יקותיאל יהודה ומרת לאה הי"ד,
marking her yahrtzeit on 10 Cheshvan

May the merit of the Torah study worldwide accompany her soul in the world of everlasting life and be a source of blessings to her family with much health, happiness, nachas, and success.

PARSHAH OVERVIEW

Vayera

G-d reveals Himself to Abraham three days after the first Jew's circumcision at age ninety-nine; but Abraham rushes off to prepare a meal for three guests who appear in the desert heat. One of the three—who are angels disguised as men—announces that, in exactly one year, the barren Sarah will give birth to a son. Sarah laughs.

Abraham pleads with G-d to spare the wicked city of Sodom. Two of the three disguised angels arrive in the doomed city, where Abraham's nephew Lot extends his hospitality to them and protects them from the evil intentions of a Sodomite mob. The two guests reveal that they have come to overturn the place and to save Lot and his family. Lot's wife turns into a pillar of salt when she disobeys the command to not look back at the burning city as they flee.

While taking shelter in a cave, Lot's two daughters (believing that they and their father are the only ones left alive in the world) get their father drunk, lie with him, and become pregnant. The two sons born from this incident father the nations of Mo'ab and Ammon.

Abraham moves to Gerar, where the Philistine king Abimelech takes Sarah—who is presented as Abraham's sister—to his palace. In a dream, G-d warns Abimelech that he will die unless he returns the woman to her husband. Abraham explains that he feared he would be killed over the beautiful Sarah.

G-d remembers His promise to Sarah and gives her and Abraham a son, who is named Isaac (Yitzchak, meaning "will laugh"). Isaac is circumcised at the age of eight days; Abraham is one hundred years old and Sarah ninety at their child's birth.

Hagar and Ishmael are banished from Abraham's home and wander in the desert; G-d hears the cry of the dying lad and saves his life by showing his mother a well.

Abimelech makes a treaty with Abraham at Beersheba, where Abraham gives him seven sheep as a sign of their truce.

INTRODUCTION

Question for Discussion

Suppose you have a friend who is very hospitable. However, there is a particular guest who drops in all the time. Your friend likes this guest and always feeds and takes care of them, but the guest takes up too much of your friend's time. They seem oblivious to how much they put your friend out and keep them from going to work. Moreover, when they chat over a meal, they often gossip, which makes your friend uncomfortable.

Your friend wants to know whether it is permissible to disinvite or stop inviting this guest.

What would you say?

The rules of understanding Rashi that we will use in our class today are:

1. Rashi only translates words if the translation is not obvious.
2. Rashi always translates words the first time they appear in the Torah.
3. Rashi only uses two explanations when each is incomplete.
4. Of the two explanations, the first will always be a better fit with the plain meaning of the text.
5. Rashi only cites the source of his translations or explanations when it helps to explain something.

I. WHO IS YOUR MASTER?

My Master

TEXT 1A

GENESIS 18:2–3

> ב. וַיָּרָץ לִקְרָאתָם מִפֶּתַח הָאֹהֶל וַיִּשְׁתַּחוּ אָרְצָה.
>
> ג. וַיֹּאמַר, אֲ-דֹנָי אִם נָא מָצָאתִי חֵן בְּעֵינֶיךָ אַל נָא תַעֲבֹר מֵעַל עַבְדֶּךָ.

2. He ran toward them from the opening of his tent and prostrated himself to the ground.

3. And he said, "My lord, If I have found favor in your eyes, please do not pass your servant by."

TEXT 1B

RASHI, AD LOC.

> לַגָּדוֹל שֶׁבָּהֶם אָמַר, וּקְרָאָם כֻּלָּם אֲדוֹנִים. וְלַגָּדוֹל אָמַר "אַל נָא תַעֲבֹר", וְכֵיוָן שֶׁלֹּא יַעֲבֹר הוּא, יַעַמְדוּ חֲבֵרָיו עִמּוֹ. וּבְלָשׁוֹן זֶה הוּא חֹל.
>
> דָּבָר אַחֵר קֹדֶשׁ הוּא, וְהָיָה אוֹמֵר לְהַקָּדוֹשׁ בָּרוּךְ הוּא לְהַמְתִּין לוֹ עַד שֶׁיָּרוּץ וְיַכְנִיס אֶת הָאוֹרְחִים...
>
> וּשְׁתֵּי הַלְּשׁוֹנוֹת בִּבְרֵאשִׁית רַבָּה.

Rabbi Shlomo Yitzchaki (Rashi)
1040–1105

Most noted biblical and Talmudic commentator. Born in Troyes, France, Rashi studied in the famed *yeshivot* of Mainz and Worms. His commentaries on the Pentateuch and the Talmud, which focus on the straightforward meaning of the text, appear in virtually every edition of the Talmud and Bible.

He was talking to the leader [of the angels], but addressed them all as lords. He addressed the words "Please do not pass your servant by" to the leader [but he intended for all three to stay]; if the leader would stay, so would his companions. According to this version, אֲדֹנָי refers to the mundane [interlocutor, not to G-d].

Another explanation: It (אֲדֹנָי) is a sacred honorific, and he was telling G-d to wait for him as he ran to tend to the wayfarers.

II. A CONFOUNDING TALE

Water and Bread

TEXT 2

GENESIS 18:4–5

> ד. יֻקַּח נָא מְעַט מַיִם וְרַחֲצוּ רַגְלֵיכֶם, וְהִשָּׁעֲנוּ תַּחַת הָעֵץ.
>
> ה. וְאֶקְחָה פַת לֶחֶם וְסַעֲדוּ לִבְּכֶם אַחַר תַּעֲבֹרוּ כִּי עַל כֵּן עֲבַרְתֶּם עַל עַבְדְּכֶם, וַיֹּאמְרוּ, כֵּן תַּעֲשֶׂה כַּאֲשֶׁר דִּבַּרְתָּ.

4. "Please let some water be taken to bathe your feet and [then] recline under the tree.

5. "And I will fetch some bread to sustain your hearts, and then you can travel onward, for [after all] you have passed by your servant." And they said, "We will do as you said."

TEXT 3

THE REBBE, RABBI MENACHEM MENDEL SCHNEERSON, *LIKUTEI SICHOT* 20, P. 69

> וויבאלד אז פאר "יוקח נא" שטייט ניט נאכאמאל "ויאמר" איז
> פארשטאנדיק, אז דאס אלץ . . . איין אמירה . . .
>
> און היות אז "יוקח נא מעט מים ורחצו רגליכם גו'" האט אברהם
> געזאגט צו די "שלשה אנשים", פארשטייט דער בן חמש למקרא
> (בפשטות), אז אויך די התחלת האמירה . . . איז געזאגט געווארן (ניט
> צום אויבערשטן, נאר) צו די "שלשה אנשים".

Rabbi Menachem Mendel Schneerson
1902–1994

The towering Jewish leader of the 20th century, known as "the Lubavitcher Rebbe," or simply as "the Rebbe." Born in southern Ukraine, the Rebbe escaped Nazi-occupied Europe, arriving in the U.S. in June 1941. The Rebbe inspired and guided the revival of traditional Judaism after the European devastation, impacting virtually every Jewish community the world over. The Rebbe often emphasized that the performance of just one additional good deed could usher in the era of Mashiach. The Rebbe's scholarly talks and writings have been printed in more than 200 volumes.

Considering that verse four does not begin with the words, "and he said," it follows that verses three and four comprise a single statement.

If the offer for water was made to the wayfarers, the five-year-old understands that the beginning of the statement was also not directed at G-d, but at the wayfarers.

In the Singular

TEXT 4

THE REBBE, RABBI MENACHEM MENDEL SCHNEERSON, IBID.

> פארוואס האט אברהם אנגעהייבן רעדן צו די "שלשה אנשים" (ניט
> בלשון רבים, נאר) בלשון יחיד?

Why didn't Abraham greet in the plural? Why did he talk to three people in singular language?

TORAH STUDIES / SEASON ONE 5785

TEXT 5A

RASHI, GENESIS 18:3

> לַגָּדוֹל שֶׁבָּהֶם אָמַר.

Abraham was talking to the leader [of the three wayfarers].

TEXT 5B

RASHI, IBID.

> וּקְרָאָם כֻּלָּם אֲדוֹנִים.

He addressed them all as lords.

TEXT 5C

RASHI, IBID.

> וְלַגָּדוֹל אָמַר אַל נָא תַעֲבֹר, וְכֵיוָן שֶׁלֹּא יַעֲבֹר הוּא יַעַמְדוּ חֲבֵרָיו עִמּוֹ.

He addressed the leader with the words, "Please do not pass by," [but he intended for all three to stay] because if the leader would stay, so would his companions.

III. PUTTING GUESTS FIRST

Who's on First?

TEXT 6A

THE REBBE, RABBI MENACHEM MENDEL SCHNEERSON, *LIKUTEI SICHOT* 25, PP. 70–71

> אין א מצב פון "וירא אליו ה'", ווי פאסט עס אז בעת מעשה זאל אברהם קוקן און דערזען "שלשה אנשים" זען בשימת לב (וועלכע ברייגגט צו וירץ לקראתם)?
>
> בשעת מען שטייט "לפני ה'" דארף דאך זיין מושלל יעדער תנועה, ועל אחת כמה וכמה שימת לב, צו א מענטשן אדער צו עפעס אן אנדער זאך!...
>
> על אחת כמה וכמה ביי אברהם וואס זיין "עומד לפני ה'" איז געווען באופן הכי גדול ונעלה... איז ווי קומט עס אז באותה שעה זאל ביי עם זיין... אז ער האט דערזען די ג' אנשים?

Abraham was in a state where "G-d revealed Himself to him." In this state, how could he look at, let alone notice, the three wayfarers? How could he pay them enough heed to be impelled to run toward them?

When standing before G-d, even a single unnecessary bodily motion is out of the question. Paying such close attention to anyone or anything is perforce proscribed.

[This would be true of anyone standing before G-d.] How much more so Abraham, whose experience of standing before G-d was so much more powerful and superior. . . . How could he at the very same time . . . notice the three wayfarers?

TEXT 6B

TALMUD, SHABBAT 127A

> אָמַר רַב יְהוּדָה אָמַר רַב: גְּדוֹלָה הַכְנָסַת אוֹרְחִין מֵהַקְבָּלַת פְּנֵי שְׁכִינָה, דִּכְתִיב: "וַיֹּאמַר ה' אִם נָא מָצָאתִי חֵן בְּעֵינֶיךָ אַל נָא תַעֲבֹר".

Rabbi Yehudah said in the name of Rav, "Hospitality is greater than hosting G-d. As the passage states, 'And he said: My lord, if I have found favor in your eyes, do not pass your servant by.'"

Babylonian Talmud

A literary work of monumental proportions that draws upon the legal, spiritual, intellectual, ethical, and historical traditions of Judaism. The 37 tractates of the Babylonian Talmud contain the teachings of the Jewish sages from the period after the destruction of the 2nd Temple through the 5th century CE. It has served as the primary vehicle for the transmission of the Oral Law and the education of Jews over the centuries; it is the entry point for all subsequent legal, ethical, and theological Jewish scholarship.

Who Told Abraham?

TEXT 7

RABBI CHAIM ALTER PANETH, *TAPUCHEI CHAYIM*, P. 18

> וְיֵשׁ לוֹמַר עַל פִּי מַה שֶׁכָּתוּב בְּסִפְרֵי הַקְּדוֹשִׁים, דְּהַצַּדִּיק מְקַדֵּשׁ אֶת אֵבָרָיו עַד שֶׁהוֹלְכִים מֵעַצְמָם לַעֲשׂוֹת רְצוֹן ה'. וּכְמוֹ שֶׁאָמַר דָּוִד הַמֶּלֶךְ: "רַגְלַי מוֹלִיכוּת אוֹתִי לְבֵית הַמִּדְרָשׁ" (סוכה כג, א).
>
> וְהִנֵּה, אַבְרָהָם אָבִינוּ - רַגְלָיו רָצוּ לִקְרַאת הָאוֹרְחִים, אַף עַל פִּי שֶׁהַשְּׁכִינָה הָיְתָה שְׁרוּיָה בְּבֵיתוֹ בְּאוֹתָהּ שָׁעָה. וּמִזֶּה הֵבִין שֶׁהַכְנָסַת אוֹרְחִים גְּדוֹלָה יוֹתֵר. וְזֶהוּ שֶׁכָּתוּב: "וַיַּרְא, וַיָּרָץ לִקְרָאתָם". פֵּירוּשׁ, רָאָה שֶׁהוּא רָץ מֵאֵלָיו לִקְרַאת הָאוֹרְחִים, וְלָמַד מִזֶּה שֶׁמִּצְוָה זוֹ גְּדוֹלָה יוֹתֵר מְקַבֶּלֶת פְּנֵי הַשְּׁכִינָה.

We can explain this based on what is written in sacred tomes: that utterly righteous people sanctify their limbs until they move spontaneously to do G-d's bidding. This is why King David said, "My feet carry me to the house of study" (Talmud, Sukkah 23a).

Rabbi Chaim Alter Paneth
1912–1984

Rabbi and author. Rabbi Chaim Alter Paneth was born in Alba Iulia (Karlsburg), Romania, where his father served as rabbi. After the Holocaust he served as the rabbi of Baia Mare, Romania, before moving to Israel where he served as a rabbi in Ramat Gan. Rabbi Paneth wrote commentaries on Mishnah Avot and on the Passover *Haggadah*, under the title *Tapuchei Chaim*.

Abraham's feet ran toward the guest, though G-d was present in his home. This told Abraham that hospitality is more important. This is the meaning of the passage, "And he saw, . . . and he ran toward them" (Genesis 18:3). He saw that he was running spontaneously toward the guest. From this, he discerned that this *mitzvah* was greater than hosting the Divine.

Yes, but Why?

TEXT 8

TALMUD, SOTAH 14A

> וְאָמַר רַבִּי חָמָא בְּרַבִּי חֲנִינָא, מַאי דִכְתִיב: "אַחֲרֵי ה' אֱלֹהֵיכֶם תֵּלֵכוּ" (דברים יג, ה), וְכִי אֶפְשָׁר לוֹ לְאָדָם לְהַלֵּךְ אַחַר שְׁכִינָה? וַהֲלֹא כְּבָר נֶאֱמַר "כִּי ה' אֱלֹקֶיךָ אֵשׁ אוֹכְלָה הוּא" (שם ד, כד).
>
> אֶלָּא, לְהַלֵּךְ אַחַר מִדּוֹתָיו שֶׁל הַקָּדוֹשׁ בָּרוּךְ הוּא: מָה הוּא מַלְבִּישׁ עֲרוּמִים . . . אַף אַתָּה הַלְבֵּשׁ עֲרוּמִים. הַקָּדוֹשׁ בָּרוּךְ הוּא בִּיקֵּר חוֹלִי . . . אַף אַתָּה בַּקֵּר חוֹלִים. הַקָּדוֹשׁ בָּרוּךְ הוּא נִיחֵם אֲבֵלִים . . . אַף אַתָּה נַחֵם אֲבֵלִים. הַקָּדוֹשׁ בָּרוּךְ הוּא קָבַר מֵתִים . . . אַף אַתָּה קְבוֹר מֵתִים.

Rabbi Chama the son of Rabbi Chanina said, "What is the meaning of the passage, 'Walk behind G-d, your G-d?' (Deuteronomy 13:5)? Is it even possible to walk behind G-d if the Torah states, 'G-d your G-d is a consuming fire' (Deuteronomy 4:24)?

"Rather, it means to emulate G-d's traits. As G-d clothes the naked, . . . so should you. As G-d visits the sick, . . . so should you. As G-d comforts the mourner, . . . so should you. As G-d buries the dead, . . . so should you."

TEXT 9

RABBI ELIYAHU MOYAL, *IMREI ELIYAHU* (HOLON, ISRAEL, 2000), P. 89

> סיבת הגדולה שבדבר מבאר בעל נתיבות שלום.
>
> לפי שאם אתה מקבל פני אוהבך בשמחה אין בזה רבותא. אבל כשאתה מקבל את בן אהובך בשמחה, ואינך שש בו ומכבדו אלא רק מפני שבנו של אוהבך הוא, הרי זה סימן מובהק לגודל אהבה השוררת ביניכם. לולא אהבתכם מה לבנו של פלוני ולך?
>
> כשיהודי בא בצל קורתך ואתה מכבדו על כי בן המלך הוא, בנו של הקדוש ברוך הוא . . . הרי זה מוכיח על אהבת ה' הבוערת בקרבך - הרבה יותר מאשר אם תקבל בכבוד את פני השכינה עצמה.

Rabbi Eliyahu Moyal

Author. Rabbi Eliyahu Moyal is a resident of Benei Berak, Israel, and he teaches at a yeshiva in Holon. He is the author of the *Imrei Eliyahu* series of books on the Bible and Talmud.

The reason why this is so great is explained by [Rabbi Boruch Sholom Berezofski, the Rebbe of Slonim and author of] *Netivot Shalom*.

If you greet your friend with joy, it doesn't demonstrate the true extent of your friendship. Greeting his child with joy, rejoicing only because it is your friend's child, demonstrates the great love you have for your friend. If not for your friendship, why would you associate with this child?

When you honor Jews in your home because they are G-d's children, . . . you demonstrate the love for G-d that burns in you, much more so than receiving G-d Himself with pomp and ceremony.

Conclusion

TEXT 10

RABBI YISRAEL BAAL SHEM TOV, *KETER SHEM TOV HASHALEM* 301:1

> עוד שמעתי ממורי הבעל שם טוב, זכר לחיי העולם הבא, ביאור "גדולה הכנסת אורחים מהקבלת פני שכינה". והקשה.
>
> והעולה, אף שלפעמים הכנסת אורחים הוא ביטול תורה, על ידי סיפורים או סיפורי לשון הרע וכו', מכל מקום, "גדולה הכנסת אורחים".

Rabbi Yisrael Baal Shem Tov (Besht)
1698–1760

Founder of the Chasidic movement. Born in Slutsk, Belarus, the Baal Shem Tov was orphaned as a child. He served as a teacher's assistant and clay digger before founding the Chasidic movement and revolutionizing the Jewish world with his emphasis on prayer, joy, and love for every Jew, regardless of his or her level of Torah knowledge.

My mentor, the Baal Shem Tov, taught me the meaning of our sages' statement that hosting our fellow is greater than hosting G-d.

He asked [since G-d doesn't reveal Himself to us, how does this statement apply to us? The answer is that we host G-d when we study the Torah].

Accordingly [the meaning of our sages' statement is this]: although hospitality prevents us sometimes from studying the Torah, and causes us to engage in idle chatter, gossip, etc., it is still the greater merit.

KEY POINTS

» There are two ways to read Abraham's opening statement. He was either addressing G-d in apology as he ran to welcome his guests, or he was addressing his guests.

» Either way, Abraham left G-d's presence to welcome guests. This teaches us that the *mitzvah* of hospitality is greater than hosting G-d.

» When we practice kindness, we emulate G-d. When we welcome a guest, we act in G-d's stead. It is like G-d is welcoming the guest through us.

» Running to welcome a guest in the middle of Torah study is like leaving G-d's presence to welcome His child. This demonstrates our ultimate love for G-d.

» The *mitzvah* of hospitality is more important than personal convenience or spiritual comfort.

Story

TEXT 11

YAEL TRUSCH, "WHY HELP OTHERS?" WWW.JHVONLINE.COM

There was once a childless Jewish couple named Eliezer and Sarah. Everyone knew of their outstanding hospitality. Once, an unkempt beggar asked to stay with them for Shabbat, and Eliezer and Sarah agreed.

The man was a handful, to say the least. He complained about everything. No matter what they gave him, he demanded more and more and had the chutzpah to get angry when they couldn't fulfill his incessant requests. He prolonged his stay beyond Shabbat, still criticizing everything.

Eliezer and Sarah continued to treat him with patience and respect despite his rude behavior. They went out of their way to make him feel as comfortable as possible.

Before he finally left, the beggar revealed himself as Eliyahu Hanavi, Elijah the prophet. He had been sent to test the couple. They passed the test admirably and, thus, would be rewarded with a son who would light up the world with his Torah and love for others.

A year later, they had a baby boy, who grew up to become the famous Rabbi Yisrael Baal Shem Tov, whose hallmark was love of every Jew.

Yael Trusch

Blogger and lecturer. A native of S. Juan, Puerto Rico, Yael Trusch received her MBA degree from NYU's Stern School of Business. She is the creator of the Jewish lifestyle blog *Jewish Latin Princess*, and she is the host of the *Jewish Money Matters* podcast.

4.
Chayei Sarah

What Do You Love about Israel?

It's More than Falafel and the IDF

Dedicated in loving memory of Mrs. Golda Kotlarsky,
מרת גאלדא בת ר' מאיר הכהן ז"ל,
marking her yahrtzeit on 19 Cheshvan

May the merit of the Torah study worldwide accompany her soul in the world of everlasting life and be a source of blessings to her family with much health, happiness, nachas, and success.

PARSHAH OVERVIEW
Chayei Sarah

Sarah dies at age 127 and is buried in the Machpelah Cave in Hebron, which Abraham purchases from Ephron the Hittite for 400 shekels of silver.

Abraham's servant Eliezer is sent, laden with gifts, to Charan, to find a wife for Isaac. At the village well, Eliezer asks G-d for a sign: when the maidens come to the well, he will ask for some water to drink; the woman who will offer to give his camels water to drink as well shall be the one destined for his master's son.

Rebecca, the daughter of Abraham's nephew Bethuel, appears at the well and passes the "test." Eliezer is invited to their home, where he repeats the story of the day's events. Rebecca returns with Eliezer to the land of Canaan, where they encounter Isaac praying in the field. Isaac marries Rebecca, loves her, and is comforted over the loss of his mother.

Abraham takes a new wife, Keturah (Hagar), and he fathers six additional sons, but Isaac is designated as his only heir. Abraham dies at age 175, and his two eldest sons, Isaac and Ishmael, bury Abraham next to Sarah.

INTRODUCTION

Question for Discussion

Many of us visit Israel whenever we can. We love it for many reasons. What makes the Land of Israel special to you?

Here are the rules we will use when reviewing this lesson's Rashi explanations:

1. Rashi only quotes words from the biblical passage he intends to address.
2. Rashi only includes explanations implied by the plain meaning of the text. Rashi does not engage in Midrashic hyperbole unless they relate to the text's plain meaning.
3. Every word in Rashi is deliberate. Words that appear to be extra or missing are always instructive.

I. THEN AND NOW

The Story

TEXT 1A

GENESIS 24:3–4

> ג. וְאַשְׁבִּיעֲךָ בַּה׳ אֱלֹקֵי הַשָּׁמַיִם וֵאלֹקֵי הָאָרֶץ, אֲשֶׁר לֹא תִקַּח אִשָּׁה לִבְנִי מִבְּנוֹת הַכְּנַעֲנִי אֲשֶׁר אָנֹכִי יוֹשֵׁב בְּקִרְבּוֹ.
>
> ד. כִּי אֶל אַרְצִי וְאֶל מוֹלַדְתִּי תֵּלֵךְ, וְלָקַחְתָּ אִשָּׁה לִבְנִי לְיִצְחָק.

3. I will have you swear by G-d, the G-d of Heaven and earth, that you will not take a woman for my son from among the daughters of the Canaanites among whom I dwell.

4. Rather, travel to my land and birthplace and take a wife for my son Isaac from there.

TEXT 1B

GENESIS 24:7

> ה׳ אֱלֹקֵי הַשָּׁמַיִם אֲשֶׁר לְקָחַנִי מִבֵּית אָבִי וּמֵאֶרֶץ מוֹלַדְתִּי, וַאֲשֶׁר דִּבֶּר לִי וַאֲשֶׁר נִשְׁבַּע לִי לֵאמֹר, לְזַרְעֲךָ אֶתֵּן אֶת הָאָרֶץ הַזֹּאת, הוּא יִשְׁלַח מַלְאָכוֹ לְפָנֶיךָ וְלָקַחְתָּ אִשָּׁה לִבְנִי מִשָּׁם.

G-d, the G-d of Heaven, Who took me from my father's home and the land of my birth, and Who spoke to me and promised to give this land to my children, will send His angel before you, and you will take a wife for my son from there.

Rashi's Comment

TEXT 2

RASHI, AD LOC.

> "ה' אֱלֹהֵי הַשָּׁמַיִם אֲשֶׁר לְקָחַנִי מִבֵּית אָבִי". וְלֹא אָמַר "וֵאלֹקֵי הָאָרֶץ", וּלְמַעְלָה אָמַר "וְאַשְׁבִּיעֲךָ וְגוֹ'?"
>
> אָמַר לוֹ: עַכְשָׁו הוּא אֱלֹקֵי הַשָּׁמַיִם וֵאלֹקֵי הָאָרֶץ, שֶׁהִרְגַּלְתִּיו בְּפִי הַבְּרִיּוֹת, אֲבָל כְּשֶׁלְּקָחַנִי מִבֵּית אָבִי הָיָה אֱלֹקֵי הַשָּׁמַיִם וְלֹא אֱלֹקֵי הָאָרֶץ, שֶׁלֹא הָיוּ בָּאֵי עוֹלָם מַכִּירִים בּוֹ, וּשְׁמוֹ לֹא הָיָה רָגִיל בָּאָרֶץ.

Rabbi Shlomo Yitzchaki (Rashi)
1040–1105

Most noted biblical and Talmudic commentator. Born in Troyes, France, Rashi studied in the famed *yeshivot* of Mainz and Worms. His commentaries on the Pentateuch and the Talmud, which focus on the straightforward meaning of the text, appear in virtually every edition of the Talmud and Bible.

"G-d, the G-d of Heaven, Who took me from my father's home." But Abraham did not add the words "and the G-d of . . . earth," whereas earlier [in verse 3] he said, "I will have you swear, etc."

Abraham told Eliezer, "Today, He is G-d of Heaven and earth because I made Him familiar in the people's lexicon. However, when He took me from my father's home, He was only the G-d of Heaven, not of earth, because humanity had yet to recognize Him, and His name was not popular on earth."

II. HERE AND THERE

The Klatz Kashye

TEXT 3

RABBI SHLOMO EPHRAIM LUNTSHITZ, *KELI YAKAR* 24:3

> שטבע האבות נמשך גם לבנים. וזה דווקא באותן עבירות הבאים מפאת החומר כאכילה וזימה וכילות וקנאה, וכל המדות הרעות הנתלין בחומר. נגעים אלו מתפשטים מהאבות לבנים, ותולדותיהן כיוצא בהם. אבל העבודת גילולים, דבר התלוי בשכלו של אדם, אינו מתפשט מאבות לבנים . . .
>
> על כן היה מרחיק הכנענים שהיו שטופי זמה, וכמה מיני עבירות הנתלים בחומר האדם, זולת עבודת גילולים, ולא הרחיק לבן ובתואל שלא היה בהם כי אם פחיתת העבודת גילולים לבד.

Rabbi Shlomo Ephraim Luntshitz
1550–1619

After studying in the yeshiva of the Maharshal, Rabbi Shlomo Ephraim gained a reputation as a distinguished preacher and scholar. He traveled far and wide to deliver his fiery sermons, which were collected and published. He is primarily known today for his work *Keli Yakar* and for his commentary on the Pentateuch, which was subsequently printed in many editions of the Bible.

The genetic nature of parents is passed down to their children. This only concerns negative habits such as overeating, lust, greed, envy, etc. that derive from our corporeal nature. Such traits are passed down to the next generation who emulate their forebears. Idol worship is different. This is the product of education, not genetic disposition. . . .

Therefore, Abraham was wary of the Canaanites, who were lustful and succumbed to sins of passion, though they refrained from idol worship. Yet, he welcomed his relatives whose only fault was idol worship.

TORAH STUDIES / SEASON ONE 5785

Answering Two Questions

TEXT 4

THE REBBE, RABBI MENACHEM MENDEL SCHNEERSON, *LIKUTEI SICHOT* 15, P. 159

> היות אז ער האט משנה געווען בלשונו - פריער "אלקי השמים ואלקי
> הארץ" און איצט נאר "אלקי השמים" - איז מובן אז אין דעם שינוי
> איז מרומז די הסברה פון אברהם צו אליעזר'ן.

Abraham adjusted his language. Earlier, he said, "G-d of Heaven and earth," and now just "G-d of Heaven." This discrepancy holds the answer to Eliezer's question.

TEXT 5A

THE REBBE, RABBI MENACHEM MENDEL SCHNEERSON, IBID.

> ווייל דאס איז נאר אן אופן "שהרגלתיו בפי הבריות" - בלויז אן
> ענין פון רגילות "בפי הבריות", אבער ניט קיין שינוי אין הנהגה און
> אין מעשה.

Because it is a superficial change, I only made G-d "familiar in the people's lexicon"—they changed their manner of speech. This did not change their habits and behavior.

Rabbi Menachem Mendel Schneerson 1902–1994

The towering Jewish leader of the 20th century, known as "the Lubavitcher Rebbe," or simply as "the Rebbe." Born in southern Ukraine, the Rebbe escaped Nazi-occupied Europe, arriving in the U.S. in June 1941. The Rebbe inspired and guided the revival of traditional Judaism after the European devastation, impacting virtually every Jewish community the world over. The Rebbe often emphasized that the performance of just one additional good deed could usher in the era of Mashiach. The Rebbe's scholarly talks and writings have been printed in more than 200 volumes.

TEXT 5B

THE REBBE, RABBI MENACHEM MENDEL SCHNEERSON, IBID.

> די השפעה פון אברהם, דער "ויקרא שם בשם ה' א-ל עולם" (בראשית כא, לג), ביז צום ווערן אויך "אלקי הארץ" (לכל הפחות אין אן אופן פון "הרגלתיו בפי"), איז ערשט געווען שפעטער נאכדעם ווי "לקחני מבית אבי". "אבל כשלקחני מבית אבי וכו' לא היה רגיל בארץ".
>
> ובמילא איז דער ארט פון "בית אבי" געווען (און געבליבן) אין אן אופן ווי ס'איז געווען נאר "אלקי השמים ולא אלקי הארץ", זיי האבן ניט מכיר געווען דעם אויבערשטן, און "שמו לא היה רגיל בארץ".

When Abraham "called out there in the name of G-d, the G-d of the world" (Genesis 21:33), G-d became the G-d of the earth (or at least part of the lexicon on earth). However, this only began [in Israel] after G-d took Abraham from his father's home. Before that time, G-d's name was not familiar on earth.

It follows that in his father's home, G-d remained as He had always been—G-d of Heaven, but not of earth. In that region, they did not recognize G-d, and His name was uncommon among them.

III. THE HOLY LAND

Direct Relationship

TEXT 6

TALMUD, KETUBOT 110B

> לְעוֹלָם יָדוּר אָדָם בְּאֶרֶץ יִשְׂרָאֵל אֲפִילוּ בְּעִיר שֶׁרוּבָּהּ גּוֹיִם, וְאַל יָדוּר בְּחוּצָה לָאָרֶץ וַאֲפִילוּ בְּעִיר שֶׁרוּבָּהּ יִשְׂרָאֵל, שֶׁכָּל הַדָּר בְּאֶרֶץ יִשְׂרָאֵל דּוֹמֶה כְּמִי שֶׁיֵּשׁ לוֹ אֱלוֹקַהּ. וְכָל הַדָּר בְּחוּצָה לָאָרֶץ דּוֹמֶה כְּמִי שֶׁאֵין לוֹ אֱלוֹקַהּ.

One should always reside in the Land of Israel, even in a city mostly populated by non-Jews, rather than outside of Israel, even in a city mostly populated by Jews. Because one who lives in the Land of Israel is considered to have a G-d. One who lives outside of the Land of Israel is considered not to have a G-d.

Babylonian Talmud

A literary work of monumental proportions that draws upon the legal, spiritual, intellectual, ethical, and historical traditions of Judaism. The 37 tractates of the Babylonian Talmud contain the teachings of the Jewish sages from the period after the destruction of the 2nd Temple through the 5th century CE. It has served as the primary vehicle for the transmission of the Oral Law and the education of Jews over the centuries; it is the entry point for all subsequent legal, ethical, and theological Jewish scholarship.

TEXT 7

RABBI DON YITZCHAK ABARBANEL, EXODUS 23:20

Rabbi Don Yitzchak Abarbanel
1437–1508

Biblical exegete and statesman. Abarbanel was born in Lisbon, Portugal, and served as a minister in the court of King Alfonso V of Portugal. After intrigues at court led to accusations against him, he fled to Spain, where he once again served as a counselor to royalty. It is claimed that Abarbanel offered King Ferdinand and Queen Isabella large sums of money for the revocation of their Edict of Expulsion of 1492, but to no avail. After the expulsion, he eventually settled in Italy, where he wrote a commentary on Scripture, as well as other venerated works.

שיש לכל אומה ואומה ועיר ועיר מזל וכוכב בשמים מורה עליו, לא ישתתף בהוראה ההיא אומה או עיר אחרת... אמנם האומה ישראלית אינה תחת ממשלת מזל וכוכב, ולא ממניעיהם, כי הוא יתברך בעצמו משגיח בהם ומשפיע עליהם... ומפני זה נקרא הקדוש ברוך הוא בערך האומות, אלקי האלקים, אבל בערך ישראל נקרא לבד אלוקה, או אלקים, או אלקי ישראל. לפי שהוא משפיע באומות על ידי אמצעיים בסדר מוגבל טבעי. והוא יתברך סבה רחוקה להם, ואלקי האלקים להם. אבל בישראל, הוא משפיע קרוב מבלי אמצעי. ולכן בערכם, נקרא אלקים בלבד, כמו שכתוב: "ואנכי אהיה להם לאלקים" (ירמיה כד, ז), ואמר: "אני ה' אלהיכם" (ויקרא כה, לח).

וכן אמרו בפרקי דרבי אלעזר (כד) על "בהנחל עליון גוים בהפרידו בני אדם" (דברים לב, ח), שבדור הפלגה באו שבעים שרים לפני הקדוש ברוך הוא והפילו גורלות על שבעים אומות. ונפל גורלו של הקדוש ברוך הוא על ישראל, שנאמר: "כי חלק ה' עמו" (שם, ט).

מפני שהיתה לארץ הנבחרת סגולה הנפלאה ויחס גדול לקבול הניצוץ האלקי, ולהיות העם היושב בה מושגח ומדובק מהקל יתברך, מבלי אמצעי, ויתר הארצות היו מונעות לזה ובלתי סובלות אותו, הוצרך יתברך לתת לישראל עמו הארץ הנבחרת. כי היא הארץ אשר "ה' דורש אותה תמיד עיני ה' בה" (דברים יא, יב)... והמקום הזה אשר בחר ה' בו נקשר בקשר אמיץ ודבקות נמרץ אלקי להשגיח ביושביו בהשגחה פרטית בלי אמצעי. מה שלא היה כן בשאר הארצות.

וכבר יראה אמתת זה מהקדושות שנמצאו בה תמיד. אם בבריאת אדם וחוה, שנבראו בה ונקברו בה. ואם ממה שצוה יתברך לאברהם שיצא מארצו וילך לדור בה, וגם כן מענין העקידה שהיה בה. וככה מהנסים הנעשים בבית המקדש תמיד, וממצוות השמיטה והיובל...

ובכלל אמרו: "ישראל הדר בחוצה לארץ כו'"... והסבה בזה, שארץ ישראל אינה תחת ממשלת שרי מעלה, כי היא מיוחדת להנהגתו יתברך. והדרים חוץ ממנה לא יונהגו באותה ההשגחה העליונה, כי אם מהנהגת השרים. וזו היא העבודת אלילים שזכרו.

The needs of every nation and city are overseen by respective angels and stars designated exclusively for them. . . . The Jewish people are not under the dominion of angels or stars; G-d oversees and provides for them by Himself. . . . Therefore, concerning other nations, G-d is called the "G-d of gods," but concerning Jews He is called "the G-d," or "G-d of Israel." This is because G-d provides for other nations via intermediaries and a finite natural order. For them, G-d is a distant cause, a G-d of gods. For Jews, G-d provides directly without intermediaries, and is, therefore, called G-d. "I will be to them for a G-d" (Jeremiah 24:7) and "I am G-d your G-d" (Leviticus 25:38).

Our sages similarly (*Pirkei Rabbi Eliezer* 24) expounded on the passage, "When G-d gave nations their lot and separated the children of Adam" (Deuteronomy 32:8). This occurred at the Tower of Babel [when G-d divided the people into seventy nations and languages]. Seventy angels appeared before G-d to draw lots over the seventy nations. G-d's lot fell upon the people of Israel, as the passage states, "For G-d's people are His portion" (Deuteronomy 32:9).

The Land of Israel has a marvelous ability to receive the spark of the Divine and to host the nation that is administered and attached directly to G-d without an intermediary. Other lands are unable to host and tolerate such intense sanctity. It was, therefore, necessary that G-d give His chosen Land to His nation Israel, the Land that He "looks after constantly; His eyes are always upon it" (Deuteronomy 11:12). . . . G-d tied His chosen Land to Him with a mighty continual Divine bond so He could oversee its inhabitants directly and with detailed providence. This is not the case with any other land.

The history of this land attests to its continual sanctity. Adam and Eve were created and buried in this land. G-d directed Abraham to leave his homeland to journey and reside in this land.

The binding of Isaac also occurred in this land. The constant miracles that occurred in the Holy Temple also took place in this land. The laws of sabbatical and jubilee [during which ordinary produce becomes sanctified, are exclusive to this land]. . . .

Our sages taught that those who live outside of Israel [are considered to have no G-d]. . . . This is because the Land of Israel is not under the dominion of the celestial ministers but exclusively directed by G-d. Those who reside outside of Israel elect not to be administered by His esoteric providence, but by the providence of angels. Thus, our sages compared it to idolatry.

Miracles

TEXT 8A

GENESIS 17:8

> נָתַתִּי לְךָ וּלְזַרְעֲךָ אַחֲרֶיךָ אֵת אֶרֶץ מְגֻרֶיךָ, אֵת כָּל אֶרֶץ כְּנַעַן לַאֲחֻזַּת עוֹלָם, וְהָיִיתִי לָהֶם לֵאלֹקִים.

I will give you and your children after you the land where you currently sojourn, the land of Canaan. And I will be to them for a G-d.

TEXT 8B

RABBI YAAKOV TZVI MECKLENBURG, *HAKETAV VEHAKABBALAH*, AD LOC.

> בביאור שם זה . . . מבואר דעת רבנו הגדול הגר"א זכרונו לברכה, כי עיקר הוראת שם זה הוא על שם השגחתו במעשי התחתונים.

To explain the choice of this name. . . . Our great teacher, Rabbi Eliyahu of blessed memory, explained that this name points primarily to G-d's direct providence over events in the terrestrial world.

Rabbi Yaakov Tzvi Mecklenburg
1785–1865

German rabbi and biblical exegete. Rabbi Yaakov served as rabbi in Königsberg, East Prussia. In 1839, he published *Haketav Vehakabbalah*, an important commentary that often demonstrates the indivisibility of the Written Torah and the Oral Torah.

TEXT 9

OPEN MIRACLE IN BE'ER SHEVA, WWW.5TOWNSCENTRAL.COM

On Friday, an "unexpected sandstorm" lasted about five minutes.

People who were standing outside recalled thinking that it was going to be a very windy Shabbat. But then, just as suddenly as it had started, it stopped. It was bizarre and seemed to come out of nowhere. However, it turns out it wasn't so random after all.

Here's what was happening in Be'er Sheva at that very moment.

Be'er Sheva hadn't heard a siren in months. The parks were full of kids on Friday, as is common before Shabbat. Suddenly, out of nowhere, a huge gust of wind hit, sending sand flying everywhere and forcing everyone to head home.

Just ten minutes later, a siren sounded. Five rockets were launched at Be'er Sheva. One landed in a playground that had been full of kids just 10 minutes earlier, causing massive damage.

That "random" gust of wind sent by [G-d] saved their lives.

All the Commandments

TEXT 10

TALMUD, SOTAH 14A

> דָּרַשׁ רַבִּי שִׂמְלַאי: מִפְּנֵי מָה נִתְאַוָּה מֹשֶׁה רַבֵּינוּ לִיכָּנֵס לְאֶרֶץ יִשְׂרָאֵל? וְכִי לֶאֱכוֹל מִפִּרְיָהּ הוּא צָרִיךְ, אוֹ לִשְׂבּוֹעַ מִטּוּבָהּ הוּא צָרִיךְ?
>
> אֶלָּא כָּךְ אָמַר מֹשֶׁה: הַרְבֵּה מִצְוֹת נִצְטַוּוּ יִשְׂרָאֵל וְאֵין מִתְקַיְּימִין אֶלָּא בְּאֶרֶץ יִשְׂרָאֵל. אֶכָּנֵס אֲנִי לָאָרֶץ כְּדֵי שֶׁיִּתְקַיְּימוּ כּוּלָּן עַל יָדִי.

Rabbi Simla'i taught, "Why did Moses yearn to enter the Land of Israel? Did he need to partake of its fruit or be satiated by its goodness?

"Rather, this is what bothered Moses. So many of the *mitzvot* that G-d gave to the Jews can only be fulfilled in the Land of Israel. [Moses said,] 'I want to enter the Land so I can fulfill them all.'"

TEXT 11

ZOHAR, VOL. 3, P. 93B

> וְקוּדְשָׁא בְּרִיךְ הוּא וּכְנֶסֶת יִשְׂרָאֵל אִקְרֵי אֶחָד, וְדָא בְּלָא דָא לָא אִקְרֵי אֶחָד . . .
>
> יִשְׂרָאֵל לְתַתָּא דְאִינּוּן . . . בְּמָה יִקְרוּן אֶחָד?
>
> בִּירוּשָׁלַיִם דִלְתַתָּא, יִקְרוּן יִשְׂרָאֵל אֶחָד.
>
> מְנָא לָן? דִכְתִיב: "גּוֹי אֶחָד בָּאָרֶץ" (שְׁמוּאֵל ב ז, כג). וַדַאי בָּאָרֶץ הֵם גּוֹי אֶחָד. עַמָּהּ אִקְרוּן אֶחָד, וְלָא אִינּוּן בִּלְחוֹדַיְיהוּ.
>
> דְּהָא "וּמִי כְעַמְּךָ יִשְׂרָאֵל". גּוֹי אֶחָד סַגִי לֵיהּ, אֲבָל לָא אִקְרוּן אֶחָד אֶלָּא בָּאָרֶץ.

Zohar

The seminal work of kabbalah, Jewish mysticism. The *Zohar* is a mystical commentary on the Torah, written in Aramaic and Hebrew. According to the Arizal, the *Zohar* contains the teachings of Rabbi Shimon bar Yocha'i, who lived in the Land of Israel during the 2nd century. The *Zohar* has become one of the indispensable texts of traditional Judaism, alongside and nearly equal in stature to the Mishnah and Talmud.

When G-d and the Jewish people are joined, they are one. Without the other, neither is one. . . .

Where are the Jewish people [joined with the] one [G-d]?

In Jerusalem.

We know this from the passage, "One nation in the Land" (II Samuel 7:23). [Read it like this:] When we are in the Land of Israel, we are one nation. In the Land of Israel, we are one. Outside the Land of Israel, we are not one.

The proof is that the passage could have sufficed with the words "one nation." [Why do the words "in the Land" appear? To teach us that] we are only one when we are in the Land of Israel.

Conclusion

TEXT 12

THE REBBE, RABBI MENACHEM MENDEL SCHNEERSON, *LIKUTEI SICHOT* 15, P. 162

> וויבאלד דאס איז געווען קודם ביטול הגזירה וואס דאמאלס
> "התחתונים יעלו לעליונים והעליונים ירדו לתחתונים" (שמות רבה
> יב, יג), וואס האט זיך אויפגעטאן בײַ מתן תורה... האט די עבודה פון
> אברהם ניט גע׳פועל׳ט א שינוי און אן עליה אין מהות פון עניני העולם
> און די בריות שבהם, אז עס זאל זיין אלקי הארץ אין אן אופן פון הכרה,
> נאר ניט מער ווי "הרגלתיו בפי הבריות".

Abraham lived before G-d gave us the Torah. At Mount Sinai, G-d removed the barrier between the celestial and terrestrial spheres, permitting "the lower sphere to ascend and the upper sphere to descend" (Midrash, *Shemot Rabah* 12:13). Abraham [who lived before this time] couldn't completely change and refine the fabric of the world and its inhabitants. He couldn't render G-d the G-d of earth by bringing people to a full [internal] recognition of G-d. He could only inspire them to speak of G-d.

TEXT 13

RABBI YOSEF YITZCHAK SCHNEERSOHN, *IGROT KODESH* 1, P. 485

> בשנת תרי"ז, שאל אחד החסידים הגדולים את הוד כבוד קדושת אבי אדוני זקני מורי ורבי, הרב הקדוש הרב צמח צדק, זכר צדיק וקדוש לברכה לחיי העולם הבא, על דבר הנסיעה לארץ ישראל, תבנה ותכונן. ויגלה לבבו כי נכסוף במאד מאד לשקוד שם בתורה ועבודה.
>
> ויענהו לאמר . . . "מיא דארף מאכין דא ארץ ישראל, מאך דא ארץ ישראל".

In 5617 (1857), one of the great Chasidim asked my saintly master and great-grandfather, Rabbi Menachem Mendel of Lubavitch, of blessed eternal memory, about traveling to Israel, may it be rebuilt and reestablished. He poured out his heart and spoke of his deep yearning to live in Israel, where he would devote his life to Torah and Divine worship.

The Rebbe replied, "We must transform *this* place into the Land of Israel. Render *this* place the Land of Israel."

Rabbi Yosef Yitzchak Schneersohn
(Rayatz, Frierdiker Rebbe, Previous Rebbe)
1880–1950

Chasidic rebbe, prolific writer, and Jewish activist. Rabbi Yosef Yitzchak, the 6th leader of the Chabad movement, actively promoted Jewish religious practice in Soviet Russia and was arrested for these activities. After his release from prison and exile, he settled in Warsaw, Poland, from where he fled Nazi occupation and arrived in New York in 1940. Settling in Brooklyn, Rabbi Schneersohn worked to revitalize American Jewish life. His son-in-law Rabbi Menachem Mendel Schneerson succeeded him as the leader of the Chabad movement.

TEXT 14

MIDRASH, *YALKUT SHIMONI*, ISAIAH 503

> אמר רבי לוי: עתידה ירושלים להיות כארץ ישראל, וארץ ישראל ככל העולם כלו.

Rabbi Levi taught, "When Mashiach comes, Jerusalem will be the size of the Land of Israel, and the Land of Israel will be the size of the entire world."

Yalkut Shimoni

A Midrash that covers the entire biblical text. Its material is collected from all over rabbinic literature, including the Babylonian and Jerusalem Talmuds and various ancient Midrashic texts. It contains several passages from *Midrashim* that have been lost, as well as different versions of existing *Midrashim*. It is unclear when and by whom this Midrash was redacted.

KEY POINTS

» Abraham wanted a daughter-in-law from among his relatives because of the pure natural traits that were common in his family.

» Yet he did not want his son to live among his relatives because they lived outside of Israel, where paganism was still rampant.

» During his years living in the Land, Abraham made the name of G-d a familiar, household name in Israel.

» This continues to be true today. G-d is more manifest, and we are more connected with G-d, in Israel than anywhere else.

» When G-d gave us the Torah, He enabled us to spread this consciousness the world over. When we complete this task, Mashiach will come. At that time, the world will be as holy as Israel is today.

5.
Toldot

It's Not So Good to Be a Goodie-Goodie
The Beauty of "The Struggle"

*Dedicated in loving memory of
Rabbi Tzvi Hirsh ben Moshe DovBer Gansbourg,
הרה"ח צבי הירש בן משה דובער ז"ל,
marking his yahrtzeit on 23 Cheshvan*

*May the merit of the Torah study worldwide accompany his soul
in the world of everlasting life and be a source of blessings to his
family with much health, happiness, nachas, and success.*

PARSHAH OVERVIEW
Toldot

Isaac and Rebecca endure twenty childless years until their prayers are answered and Rebecca conceives. She experiences a difficult pregnancy as the "children struggle inside her"; G-d tells her that "there are two nations in your womb," and that the younger will prevail over the elder.

Esau emerges first; Jacob is born clutching Esau's heel. Esau grows up to be "a cunning hunter, a man of the field"; Jacob is "a wholesome man," a dweller in the tents of learning. Isaac favors Esau; Rebecca loves Jacob. Returning exhausted and hungry from the hunt one day, Esau sells his birthright (his rights as the firstborn) to Jacob for a pot of red lentil stew.

In Gerar, in the land of the Philistines, Isaac presents Rebecca as his sister out of fear that he will be killed by someone coveting her beauty. He farms the land, reopens the wells dug by his father, Abraham, and digs a series of his own wells. Over the first two there is strife with the Philistines, but the waters of the new wells are enjoyed in tranquility.

Esau marries two Hittite women. Isaac grows old and blind and expresses his desire to bless Esau before he dies. While Esau goes off to hunt for his father's favorite food, Rebecca dresses Jacob in Esau's clothes, covers his arms and neck with goatskins to simulate the feel of his hairier brother, prepares a similar dish, and sends Jacob to his father. Jacob receives his father's blessings for "the dew of the heaven and the fat of the land" and mastery over his brother. When Esau returns and the deception is revealed, all Isaac can do for his weeping son is predict that he will live by his sword, and that when Jacob falters, the younger brother will forfeit his supremacy over the elder.

Jacob leaves home for Haran to flee Esau's wrath and to find a wife in the family of his mother's brother, Laban. Esau marries a third wife—Mahalath, the daughter of Ishmael.

INTRODUCTION

The rules we will use to examine this lesson's Rashi explanations are:

1. When a discrepancy arises between two texts, Rashi explains it in the latter instance—when the discrepancy comes to light and the question arises. He does not address it in the first instance before the discrepancy comes to light.

2. Although there are strict grammatical rules for Hebrew spelling, many of them do not impact the text's plain meaning. Rashi does not address grammatical discrepancies (like *male* vs. *chaser*) that don't impact the text's plain meaning.

3. Rashi addresses such discrepancies if they impact matters pertaining to the text's plain meaning.

4. Rashi's words contain the "wine of Torah"—ideas and messages from the kabbalistic/Chasidic dimension of the Torah.

I. WHAT'S IN A WORD?

Textual Discrepancies

TEXT 1

GENESIS 25:24

> וַיִּמְלְאוּ יָמֶיהָ לָלֶדֶת, וְהִנֵּה תוֹמִם בְּבִטְנָהּ.

And her days to give birth were completed, and behold, there were twins in her womb.

TEXT 2A

RASHI, AD LOC.

> "וַיִּמְלְאוּ יָמֶיהָ". אֲבָל בְּתָמָר כְּתִיב: "וַיְהִי בְּעֵת לִדְתָּהּ" (בְּרֵאשִׁית לח, כז). שֶׁלֹּא מָלְאוּ יָמֶיהָ, כִּי לְז' חֳדָשִׁים יְלָדָתַם.

"And her days . . . were completed." But regarding Tamar, the passage phrases it differently: "And it came about when she gave birth [and behold there were twins in her womb]" (Genesis 38:27). This is because [Tamar's] pregnancy term was not filled; she gave birth to them after seven months.

Rabbi Shlomo Yitzchaki (Rashi)
1040–1105

Most noted biblical and Talmudic commentator. Born in Troyes, France, Rashi studied in the famed *yeshivot* of Mainz and Worms. His commentaries on the Pentateuch and the Talmud, which focus on the straightforward meaning of the text, appear in virtually every edition of the Talmud and Bible.

LESSON 5 / IT'S NOT SO GOOD TO BE A GOODIE-GOODIE

TEXT 2B

RASHI, AD LOC.

> "וְהִנֵּה תוֹמִם". חָסֵר. וּבְתָמָר תְּאוֹמִים מָלֵא, לְפִי שֶׁשְּׁנֵיהֶם צַדִּיקִים, אֲבָל כָּאן אֶחָד צַדִּיק וְאֶחָד רָשָׁע.

"There were twins in her womb." [תוֹמִם, the word for twins, is spelled] defectively [missing an *alef* and *yud*]. Tamar's [twins] are described as תְּאוֹמִים—with the complete spelling [including the *alef* and *yud*]. This is because Tamar's twins were both righteous, but in this case, one was virtuous, and one was wicked.

Two Questions

TEXT 3

THE REBBE, RABBI MENACHEM MENDEL SCHNEERSON, *LIKUTEI SICHOT* 30, P. 110

> נתבאר כמה פעמים, שכאשר ישנה סתירה בין שני כתובים, דרכו של רש"י ליישבה בכתוב השני, במקום שמתעוררת הסתירה.
>
> ואם כן קשה בנדון דידן - מה ראה רש"י לעמוד כאן על השינוי בין לשון הכתוב כאן ולשון הכתוב לקמן בתמר?

We explained many times that when there is a discrepancy between two passages, Rashi's method is to resolve it in the second passage, where the discrepancy arises.

This raises a question: Why does Rashi address the discrepancy between this passage and the later passage at this [earlier] point?

Rabbi Menachem Mendel Schneerson 1902–1994

The towering Jewish leader of the 20th century, known as "the Lubavitcher Rebbe," or simply as "the Rebbe." Born in southern Ukraine, the Rebbe escaped Nazi-occupied Europe, arriving in the U.S. in June 1941. The Rebbe inspired and guided the revival of traditional Judaism after the European devastation, impacting virtually every Jewish community the world over. The Rebbe often emphasized that the performance of just one additional good deed could usher in the era of Mashiach. The Rebbe's scholarly talks and writings have been printed in more than 200 volumes.

TEXT 4

THE REBBE, RABBI MENACHEM MENDEL SCHNEERSON, IBID., P. 111

> נתבאר כמה פעמים, וכן כתבו כמה מפרשי רש"י, שהשינויים ד"מלא" ו"חסר" כשלעצמם אינם ענין המעורר קושי בפשוטו של מקרא (שלכן על פי רוב אין רש"י מבאר הטעם לחסרות כו' שבמקרא), ובמקום שרש"י מבאר טעמם, הרי זה רק משום שעל ידי זה מתבאר דבר הקשה בפשוטו של מקרא.
>
> ועל פי זה יש להבין בנידון דידן - מה קשה בלשון הכתוב "והנה תומים בבטנה" שבגלל זה מדייק רש"י ש"תומם" חסר כתיב?

We explained many times, and several supercommentaries to Rashi agree, that Rashi does not ordinarily address defective spellings because they don't impact the text's plain meaning. On the rare occasions when Rashi addresses them, it is only because the unusual spelling resolves a difficulty in the text.

This raises the question: What is the difficulty in the words "behold, there were twins in her womb" that compels Rashi to address the defective spelling?

LESSON 5 / IT'S NOT SO GOOD TO BE A GOODIE-GOODIE

II. WHO CARES?

A Local Problem

TEXT 5

THE REBBE, RABBI MENACHEM MENDEL SCHNEERSON,
LIKUTEI SICHOT 30, PP. 111–112

> לולא הכתוב כאן "וימלאו ימיה" (ברבקה), לא היינו יודעים לדייק שהכוונה בתיבות "בעת לדתה" (בתמר) היא "לחסרים" (והיינו מפרשים הכתוב כפשוטו, שרק בעת לדתה נודעה לתמר שתאומים בבטנה).
>
> אבל לאחר שנאמר ברבקה הלשון "וימלאו ימיה", מה שאין כן בתמר כתיב "ויהי בעת לדתה". . . הרי שינוי זה שבין הכתובים מלמדנו, שבתמר "לא מלאו ימיה".

If not for the passage "And her days were completed" about Rebecca, we would not have known that the words "when she gave birth" about Tamar tell us that it was less than nine months. We would have understood it to mean that Tamar only discovered she was carrying twins at birth.

Now that the Torah says "And her days were completed" about Rebecca and "when she gave birth" about Tamar, we see the discrepancy. This tells us that Tamar's pregnancy did not last for nine months.

Yes, but Why?

TEXT 6

THE REBBE, RABBI MENACHEM MENDEL SCHNEERSON, IBID., P. 112

> וכדי ליישב שאלות אלו ממשיך רש"י בדיבור המתחיל שלאחרי זה "והנה תומם - חסר, ובתמר תאומים מלא לפי ששניהם צדיקים, אבל כאן אחד צדיק ואחד רשע".
>
> כלומר: לאחרי שרואים שהכתוב מחלק בין שתי הלידות דרבקה ותמר כדי ללמד שזו למלאים וזו לחסרים, מסתבר לומר שיש להשוות ולדייק גם בשאר השינויים שביניהם.
>
> שכאן כתיב "תומם חסר, ובתמר תאומים מלא" - כי בזה מודגש, שכל כוונת הכתוב כאן היא להשוות את שתי הלידות ולהדגיש את השינויים ביניהן, דאף ששתיהן ילדו תאומים, מכל מקום היה שינוי עיקרי ביניהן.

To resolve these questions, Rashi continues with the following comment: "Here, the word 'twins' is spelled in defective form. Concerning Tamar, it is spelled in complete form because [her twins] were both righteous. However, in this case, one was righteous, and the other was wicked."

Rashi's meaning: once we see that the Torah contrasts the two births to teach us that one was brought to complete term and the other was not, it follows that we should compare and contrast all the discrepancies between them.

The reason the word "twins" is spelled in defective form here and in complete form there should also be examined. The purpose is to compare the two births and highlight their differences. Though both gave birth to twins, they had some essential differences.

TEXT 7

RABBI YISACHAR BER EILENBURG, *TZEDAH LADERECH*, GENESIS 38:27

> והטעם, לפי שמיהר הקדוש ברוך הוא להביא שני צדיקים בעולם הזה.

The reason is simple: G-d hastened to bring two righteous people to the world.

Rabbi Yissachar Ber Eilenburg
c. 1550–1623

Halachic authority and Bible commentator. Born in Poznan, Poland, Rabbi Eilenburg studied under the famous Halachists Rabbi Mordechai Yaffe and Rabbi Yehoshua Falk and went on to serve as the rabbi of Gorizia, Italy. He is known for *Beer Sheva*, a work including Talmudic commentary and Halachic responsa; and *Tzedah Laderech*, a supercommentary to Rashi's classic biblical commentary.

III. WHAT CHALLENGES REVEAL

In the Womb

TEXT 8

MIDRASH, *BERESHIT RABAH* 63:6

> בְּשָׁעָה שֶׁהָיְתָה עוֹמֶדֶת עַל בָּתֵּי כְנֵסִיּוֹת וּבָתֵּי מִדְרָשׁוֹת, יַעֲקֹב מְפַרְכֵּס לָצֵאת . . . וּבְשָׁעָה שֶׁהָיְתָה עוֹבֶרֶת עַל בָּתֵּי עֲבוֹדַת כּוֹכָבִים, עֵשָׂו רָץ וּמְפַרְכֵּס לָצֵאת.

When Rebecca stood near a synagogue or house of Torah study, Jacob struggled to emerge. When she passed a house of pagan worship, Esau struggled to emerge.

Bereshit Rabah

An early rabbinic commentary on the Book of Genesis. This Midrash bears the name of Rabbi Oshiya Rabah (Rabbi Oshiya "the Great"), whose teaching opens this work. This Midrash provides textual exegeses and stories, expounds upon the biblical narrative, and develops and illustrates moral principles. Produced by the sages of the Talmud in the Land of Israel, its use of Aramaic closely resembles that of the Jerusalem Talmud. It was first printed in Constantinople in 1512 together with 4 other Midrashic works on the other 4 books of the Pentateuch.

Natural Tendencies

TEXT 9A

MAIMONIDES, *SHEMONAH PERAKIM*, INTRODUCTION TO AVOT, CHAPTER 6

> אמרו הפילוסופים, שהמושל בנפשו, אף על פי שעשה המעשים הטובים והחשובים, הוא עושה אותם והוא מתאוה אל הפעולות הרעות ונכסף אליהם, ויכבוש את יצרו . . . ויעשה הטובות והוא מצטער בעשיתם.
>
> אבל החסיד הוא נמשך בפעולתו אחר מה שתעירהו אליו תאותו ותכונתו. ויעשה הטובות והוא מתאוה ונכסף אליהן.

The philosophers maintain [that there are two personalities]: those whose deeds are good and important, but who crave and desire terrible things. They subdue their inclinations and rein in their desires.

Rabbi Moshe ben Maimon (Maimonides, Rambam)
1135–1204

Halachist, philosopher, author, and physician. Maimonides was born in Córdoba, Spain. After the conquest of Córdoba by the Almohads, he fled Spain and eventually settled in Cairo, Egypt. There, he became the leader of the Jewish community and served as court physician to the vizier of Egypt. He is most noted for authoring the *Mishneh Torah*, an encyclopedic arrangement of Jewish law; and for his philosophical work, *Guide for the Perplexed*. His rulings on Jewish law are integral to the formation of Halachic consensus.

LESSON 5 / IT'S NOT SO GOOD TO BE A GOODIE-GOODIE

Then there are the pious ones. Their good behavior is stimulated by their desires and inclinations. They perform good deeds because they crave and desire them.

Question for Discussion

Of the two, whose path is more virtuous?

TEXT 9B

MAIMONIDES, IBID.

> ובהסכמה מן הפילוסופים שהחסיד יותר חשוב ויותר שלם מן המושל בנפשו. אבל אמרו אפשר שיהיה המושל בנפשו כחסיד בענינים רבים, ומעלתו למטה ממנו בהכרח, להיותו מתאוה לפועל הרע. ואף על פי שאינו עושה אותו מפני שתשוקתו לרע, היא תכונה רעה בנפש.
>
> וכאשר חקרנו דברי חכמים בזה הענין, נמצא להם שהמתאוה לעבירות והנכסף אליהם יותר חשוב ויותר שלם מאשר לא מתאוה אליהם, ולא יצטער בהנחתם. עד שאמרו, שכל אשר יהיה האיש יותר חשוב ויותר שלם, תהיה תשוקתו לעבירות והצטערו בהנחתן יותר גדול... ולא דים זה, אלא שאמרו ששכר המושל בנפשו גדול לפי רוב צערו במשלו בנפשו.

The consensus among philosophers is that the pious are more praiseworthy and perfect than those who rein in their passions. The latter might be identical to the righteous in behavior, yet they are of lower stature due to their negative tendencies. Even if they don't surrender to these tendencies, these tendencies stain their souls.

Yet, when we examine the words of our wise sages, we find that those tempted to sin are more praiseworthy and complete than those with no sinful cravings. They went so far as to say that the more perfect and complete one is, the more desirous of sin one becomes, and the more difficult it becomes for one to overcome those desires. . . . Moreover, they said our reward is commensurate with how difficult it is for us to resist our tendencies.

Brute Power

TEXT 10

RABBI SHALOM DOVBER SCHNEERSOHN, *SEFER HAMAAMARIM* 5646–5650, P. 186

> אמרו רבותינו זכרונם לברכה: "אין הקדוש ברוך הוא בא בטרוניא עם בריותיו" (עבודה זרה ג, א).
>
> ומזה יובן שמה שניתן לישראל תורה ומצוות, אין זה יותר מכפי כוחן. דהגם דתורה ומצוות לקיים כדבעי למהוי היא עבודה עצומה, ומכל מקום ניתן לישראל לקיימם, דדוקא נשמות ישראל יש בהם כח זה לקיים המצוות.

Rabbi Shalom Dovber Schneersohn (Rashab)
1860–1920

Chasidic rebbe. Rabbi Shalom Dovber became the 5th leader of the Chabad movement upon the passing of his father, Rabbi Shmuel Schneersohn. He established the Lubavitch network of *yeshivot* called Tomchei Temimim. He authored many volumes of Chasidic discourses and is renowned for his lucid and thorough explanations of kabbalistic concepts.

Our sages of blessed memory said, "G-d makes no unfair demands of His creations" (Talmud, Avodah Zarah 3a).

From this, we infer that the Torah and *mitzvot* that G-d gave us are not beyond our capacity. Though it is tough to comply correctly with all the Torah's requirements, the Torah was, nevertheless, given to us because we can live up to the challenge.

LESSON 5 / IT'S NOT SO GOOD TO BE A GOODIE-GOODIE

KEY POINTS

» Some people are born with the capacity to be righteous, and others with the capacity to be wicked. This doesn't mean they will be that way: just that they can.

» Most parents prefer that their children be among the former. However, there is one benefit to being among the latter.

» The capacity to be wicked comes with the resources to overcome temptation.

» G-d never asks of us what we can't deliver. If He challenges us, it means He gave us the ability to overcome the challenge.

» This means that a child with the capacity to be wicked has greater inner resources than one born righteous. To access and activate these resources, this child requires a challenge. But once challenged, their innate strengths emerge.

6.
Vayetze

Jacob's Moral Dilemma

Don't Be Pious at Someone Else's Expense

Dedicated to Lou and Claire D'Angelo in appreciation for their friendship and partnership with JLI and their dedication to bringing the light of Torah to communities across the globe

PARSHAH OVERVIEW
Vayetze

Jacob leaves his hometown of Be'er Sheba and journeys to Charan. On the way, he encounters "the place" and sleeps there, dreaming of a ladder connecting Heaven and earth, with angels climbing and descending on it; G-d appears and promises that the land upon which he lies will be given to his descendants. In the morning, Jacob raises the stone on which he laid his head as an altar and monument, pledging that it will be made the house of G-d.

In Charan, Jacob stays with and works for his uncle Laban, tending Laban's sheep. Laban agrees to give him his younger daughter, Rachel—whom Jacob loves—in marriage, in return for seven years' labor. But on the wedding night, Laban gives him his elder daughter, Leah, instead—a deception Jacob discovers only in the morning.

Jacob marries Rachel, too, a week later, after agreeing to work another seven years for Laban.

Leah gives birth to six sons—Reuben, Simeon, Levi, Judah, Issachar, and Zebulun—and a daughter, Dinah, while Rachel remains barren. Rachel gives Jacob her handmaiden, Bilhah, as a wife to bear children in her stead, and two more sons, Dan and Naphtali, are born. Leah does the same with her handmaiden, Zilpah, who gives birth to Gad and Asher. Finally, Rachel's prayers are answered and she gives birth to Joseph.

Jacob has now been in Charan for fourteen years, and wishes to return home. But Laban persuades him to remain, now offering him sheep in return for his labor. Jacob prospers despite Laban's repeated attempts to swindle him. After six years, Jacob leaves Charan in stealth, fearing that Laban will prevent him from leaving with the family and property for which he labored. Laban pursues Jacob but is warned by G-d in a dream not to harm him. Laban and Jacob make a pact on Mount Gal-Ed, attested to by a pile of stones, and Jacob proceeds to the Holy Land, where he is met by angels.

INTRODUCTION

Questions for Discussion

1. *Should you take a six-month hiatus from Torah Studies to teach your neighbor Hebrew, or should you continue your classes until your neighbor can free up another timeslot?*

2. *Is your spiritual growth more or less important than your neighbor's spiritual growth? Support your position.*

The rules that we will use to analyze Rashi's approach:

1. If there is a difficulty in the text that would bother a five-year-old student, Rashi addresses it.

2. If Rashi does not address it, it can mean one of two things: either (a) it's not a question, or (b) the answer is obvious from Rashi's previous comments.

I. A STRANGE MARRIAGE

Two Sisters

TEXT 1A

GENESIS 29:16

> וּלְלָבָן שְׁתֵּי בָנוֹת, שֵׁם הַגְּדֹלָה לֵאָה וְשֵׁם הַקְּטַנָּה רָחֵל.

And Laban had two daughters. The older one was Leah, and the younger one was Rachel.

TEXT 1B

GENESIS 29:23

> וַיְהִי בָעֶרֶב, וַיִּקַּח אֶת לֵאָה בִתּוֹ וַיָּבֵא אֹתָהּ אֵלָיו, וַיָּבֹא אֵלֶיהָ.

And it was in the evening, and he [Laban] took his daughter Leah and brought her to him. And he married her.

TEXT 1C

GENESIS 29:30

> וַיָּבֹא גַּם אֶל רָחֵל, וַיֶּאֱהַב גַּם אֶת רָחֵל מִלֵּאָה.

And he also married Rachel, and he loved Rachel more than Leah.

TEXT 2

LEVITICUS 18:18

> וְאִשָּׁה אֶל אֲחֹתָהּ לֹא תִקָּח, לִצְרֹר לְגַלּוֹת עֶרְוָתָהּ עָלֶיהָ בְּחַיֶּיהָ.

Do not take a woman [in marriage] with her sister as rivals, to uncover the nakedness of one upon the other in her lifetime.

TEXT 3A

GENESIS 26:5

> אֲשֶׁר שָׁמַע אַבְרָהָם בְּקֹלִי וַיִּשְׁמֹר מִשְׁמַרְתִּי.

Abraham hearkened to My voice and kept My charge.

TEXT 3B

RASHI, AD LOC.

> "וַיִּשְׁמֹר מִשְׁמַרְתִּי". גְּזֵרוֹת לְהַרְחָקָה עַל הָאַזְהָרוֹת שֶׁבַּתּוֹרָה, כְּגוֹן שְׁנִיּוֹת לָעֲרָיוֹת.

"He kept My charge." [Referring to] decrees to distance oneself from actions that the Torah warns against. For example, prohibitions to prevent illicit relationships.

Rabbi Shlomo Yitzchaki (Rashi)
1040–1105

Most noted biblical and Talmudic commentator. Born in Troyes, France, Rashi studied in the famed *yeshivot* of Mainz and Worms. His commentaries on the Pentateuch and the Talmud, which focus on the straightforward meaning of the text, appear in virtually every edition of the Talmud and Bible.

II. NOT ON HER ACCOUNT

The Noahide Code—a Binding Law

TEXT 4

MAIMONIDES, *MISHNEH TORAH*, LAWS OF KINGS AND WAR 9:1

> עַל שִׁשָּׁה דְּבָרִים נִצְטַוָּה אָדָם הָרִאשׁוֹן: עַל עֲבוֹדָה זָרָה, וְעַל בִּרְכַּת הַשֵּׁם, וְעַל שְׁפִיכוּת דָּמִים, וְעַל גִּלּוּי עֲרָיוֹת, וְעַל הַגֵּזֶל, וְעַל הַדִּינִים.
>
> אַף עַל פִּי שֶׁכֻּלָּן הֵן קַבָּלָה בְּיָדֵינוּ מִמֹּשֶׁה רַבֵּנוּ, וְהַדַּעַת נוֹטָה לָהֶן, מִכְּלַל דִּבְרֵי תּוֹרָה יֵרָאֶה שֶׁעַל אֵלּוּ נִצְטַוָּה.
>
> הוֹסִיף לְנֹחַ אֵבֶר מִן הַחַי, שֶׁנֶּאֱמַר: "אַךְ בָּשָׂר בְּנַפְשׁוֹ דָמוֹ לֹא תֹאכֵלוּ" (בְּרֵאשִׁית ט, ד).
>
> נִמְצְאוּ שֶׁבַע מִצְווֹת.

Rabbi Moshe ben Maimon (Maimonides, Rambam)
1135–1204

Halachist, philosopher, author, and physician. Maimonides was born in Córdoba, Spain. After the conquest of Córdoba by the Almohads, he fled Spain and eventually settled in Cairo, Egypt. There, he became the leader of the Jewish community and served as court physician to the vizier of Egypt. He is most noted for authoring the *Mishneh Torah*, an encyclopedic arrangement of Jewish law; and for his philosophical work, *Guide for the Perplexed*. His rulings on Jewish law are integral to the formation of Halachic consensus.

Adam was given six commandments: The prohibitions against idol worship, blasphemy, murder, incest and adultery, and theft, as well as the commandment to establish courts of justice.

Though we received these commandments [separately] from Moses and [we would have embraced them regardless because] they are logical, it still appears from the Torah that G-d instructed Adam concerning them.

G-d added the prohibition against eating flesh from a living animal and gave it to Noah. As it is written, "You may not eat flesh with its life, which is its blood" (Genesis 9:4).

Thus, there are seven commandments.

Additional Binding Laws: Honoring Parents

TEXT 5

RASHI, GENESIS 11:32

> כְּשֶׁיָּצָא אַבְרָם מֵחָרָן עֲדַיִן נִשְׁאֲרוּ מִשְּׁנוֹתָיו הַרְבֵּה, וְלָמָה הִקְדִּים הַכָּתוּב מִיתָתוֹ שֶׁל תֶּרַח לִיצִיאָתוֹ שֶׁל אַבְרָם?
>
> שֶׁלֹּא יְהֵא הַדָּבָר מְפֻרְסָם לַכֹּל, וְיֹאמְרוּ: לֹא קִיֵּם אַבְרָם אֶת כְּבוֹד אָבִיו.

Terah lived for many years after Abraham left Charan, so why did the Torah relate Terah's death before Abraham's departure?

So that the matter would not become public knowledge and people would not gossip that Abraham failed to fulfill the requirement to honor one's father.

Additional Binding Law: Illicit Relations

TEXT 6

RASHI, GENESIS 34:7

> לַעֲנוֹת אֶת הַבְּתוּלוֹת, שֶׁהָאֻמּוֹת גָּדְרוּ עַצְמָן מִן הָעֲרָיוֹת עַל יְדֵי הַמַּבּוּל.

Rape was proscribed when the nations adopted laws against all illicit relationships as a result of the flood.

The Power to Overrule

TEXT 7

RABBI YAKOV HEIZLER, *RAV RABANAN AL MARAN BAAL SHEVET HALEVI*, P. 401

> כמה פעמים שינן לפני המשמשים בהוראה, שבעל הוראה, אף על פי שדעתו נוטה בדרך כלל לחומרה, מכל מקום, צריך לדעת מהי שורת הדין ומה חומרא, כדי שבבא שאלה לפניו ידע להקל במקום הצורך.

[Rabbi Shmuel Wosner] often reminded rabbis who serve as Halachic decisors to know which stringencies are Halachically binding and which are motivated by one's personal scruples. This way, even rabbis who are inclined to be stringent will know when it is necessary to rule leniently.

Honesty—Another Binding Law

TEXT 8

GENESIS 29:25

> וַיְהִי בַבֹּקֶר, וְהִנֵּה הִיא לֵאָה. וַיֹּאמֶר אֶל לָבָן: "מַה זֹּאת עָשִׂיתָ לִּי! הֲלֹא בְרָחֵל עָבַדְתִּי עִמָּךְ, וְלָמָּה רִמִּיתָנִי?"

And it was in the morning and behold it was Leah. And he said to Laban, "What is this that you did to me?! Behold I worked for you for the right to marry Rachel. And why did you deceive me?"

LESSON 6 / JACOB'S MORAL DILEMMA

TEXT 9A

THE REBBE, RABBI MENACHEM MENDEL SCHNEERSON, *LIKUTEI SICHOT* 5, P. 147

> פון די זהירות'ן וואס זיינען דעמאלט געווארן אנגענומען ביי די אומות,
> איז געווען - צו אפהיטן זיך פון אפנארן איינער דעם אנדערן.
>
> וכדמוכח פון דעם וואס יעקב האט גע'טענה'ט צו לבן "ולמה
> רמיתני" (בראשית כט, כה), ביז אפילו לבן (הרמאי) האט געמוזט
> פארענטפערן זיך מיט דער בארעכטיקונג, אז "לא יעשה כן במקומינו
> גו'" (שם, כו).

Rabbi Menachem Mendel Schneerson
1902–1994

The towering Jewish leader of the 20th century, known as "the Lubavitcher Rebbe," or simply as "the Rebbe." Born in southern Ukraine, the Rebbe escaped Nazi-occupied Europe, arriving in the U.S. in June 1941. The Rebbe inspired and guided the revival of traditional Judaism after the European devastation, impacting virtually every Jewish community the world over. The Rebbe often emphasized that the performance of just one additional good deed could usher in the era of Mashiach. The Rebbe's scholarly talks and writings have been printed in more than 200 volumes.

One of the norms adopted at that time by the nations was to refrain from deception.

This may be inferred from Jacob's demand of Laban, "Why did you deceive me?" (Genesis 29:25). [This norm was accepted] to the extent that even Laban the swindler was compelled to defend himself with the argument that [marrying the younger sister ahead of the older sister] "is not done in our place" (Genesis 29:26).

Competing Obligations

TEXT 9B

THE REBBE, RABBI MENACHEM MENDEL SCHNEERSON, IBID., PP. 147–148

> ווייל יעקב האט פריער צוגעזאגט חתונה צו האבן מיט רחל'ען ... איז
> אויב ער וואלט איר ניט דערפילט דעם צוזאג, וואלט ער דאך דערמיט
> באגאנגען רמייה.
>
> במילא איז מובן, אז די חומרא פון אפהיטן דעם לאו "ואשה אל
> אחותה לא תקח" (ויקרא יח, יח), אויף וועלכען ס'איז דאן ניט געווען
> קיין ציווי, האט ניט געקענט דוחה זיין דעם איסור פון רמייה.

Considering that Jacob had previously promised Rachel that he would marry her, . . . not keeping his pledge would have been deceptive.

His personal choice to observe the nonbinding stringency "Do not take a woman and her sister" (Leviticus 18:18) could not overrule the prohibition against deception.

III. THE WINE OF TORAH: OTHERS FIRST

Luxury vs. Necessity

TEXT 10

THE REBBE, RABBI MENACHEM MENDEL SCHNEERSON, IBID., P. 148

> בשעת ס'איז דא א איד וואס ווייס ניט פון אידישקייט, און מען דארף
> אים געבן צדקה ברוחניות, דערצייל‍ן אים און ווייזן אים די וועג פון
> אידישקייט וכו', האט א צווייטער איד... קיין רעכט ניט צי טענה'ן אז
> ער וועט בעסער אט די צייט פארנוצן פאר זיך אויף צו שטייגן אליין
> אין תורה ועבודה.
>
> נאר ער דארף זיך אליין משפט'ן: מיט וואס איז ער דאס וויכטיקער
> און שענער פון יענעם, אז ער דארף האבן כל מיני הידורים ברוחניות,
> אויפן חשבון פון דעם וואס ער וועט פארמיידן פון א צווייטן אידן די
> ענינים הכי מוכרחים?

Some Jews know nothing of Judaism and require spiritual charity—someone to teach and show them the basics. In such circumstances, no one has the right to claim they can't because their time would be better utilized studying Torah and praying.

Rather we must judge ourselves: What makes our spiritual devotions more important or better than those of our fellow? Is it right for us to worship G-d at the highest level, at the price of refusing other Jews their basic spiritual needs?

Giving Your Time

TEXT 11

JEWISH EDUCATIONAL MEDIA, MR. SHIMSHON STOCK, "IN-REACH," *LIVING TORAH*, 72:286, WWW.CHABAD.ORG

I was a crazy kid. I was wild. At one point, my friend was serving the Previous Rebbe, and I was sitting upstairs and rushing him to serve [the Rebbe] faster. I said, "Hurry up, we have to go."

So, the Rebbe asked, "What is your rush? Where are you going?"

I said, "You don't want to know."

He said, "Tell me. I won't tell anyone."

I said, "You don't want to know."

I had just turned fifteen. After he asked several times, I told him. I did not have the nerve to tell him right away that I wanted to go to the movies. But since he said, "Tell me. I won't feel bad; I won't tell anyone," I told him.

The Rebbe asked, "Maybe, instead of rushing [to go to the movies], I will learn Torah with you for half an hour, from 8:00 to 8:30?"

We went to learn with him every Thursday night for about six weeks. . . . I was not studious; I was not interested in it. So, we sat and discussed, and he would encourage me to be more observant. He would not rebuke me. Rather, he helped me understand that it would be better for me to be more observant.

We studied the abridged Code of Jewish Law, that much I recall. But we did not delve into it deeply. We learned certain laws, but we did not discuss them much; he focused more on my character traits. He did not lower my self-esteem; he did not push me down. He never pushed people down. Especially me; I don't know why, but that was the Rebbe. He never pushed people down.

Your Inner Voice

TEXT 12

RABBI DR. TZVI HERSH WEINREB, "A JEW FROM MARYLAND," JEMEDIA.ORG, JUNE 8, 2013

And then I heard the Rebbe say in the background, in Yiddish: "Tell him that there is a Jew who lives in Maryland that he can speak to. *Der Yid hayst Veinreb*—his name is Weinreb."

The secretary asked me, "Did you hear what the Rebbe said?"

Now, I couldn't believe my ears. I knew for sure I had not given the secretary my name, but the Rebbe had just said my name. I was taken aback, and I wanted to hear it again. So, when the secretary asked whether I heard, I said no. The secretary repeated the Rebbe's words to me: "*S'iz doh a Yid in Maryland mit vemen er zol redden. Zayn numen iz Veinreb.*" "There's a Jew in Maryland with whom he should speak. His name is Weinreb."

So, I replied, "But my name is Weinreb!"

And then I heard the Rebbe say, "*Oib azoi, zol er visen zayn az amol darf men reden tzu zich*—if that's the case, then he should know that, sometimes, one needs to speak to himself."

The secretary also seemed stunned by what was taking place. He just stopped, and I could hear his breathing. And then he said to me, "The Rebbe said that sometimes it's best to talk to yourself. Isn't your name Weinreb?"

"Yes, my name is Weinreb, but maybe the Rebbe means a different Weinreb?"

Rabbi Dr. Tzvi Hersh Weinreb 1940–

Psychotherapist, writer, and orator. Rabbi Weinreb received his rabbinic ordination from the Rabbi Jacob Joseph Yeshiva in New York and earned his PhD from the University of Maryland. He is currently the executive vice president emeritus of the Orthodox Union.

"No, the Rebbe's saying, 'Talk to Weinreb,' and he explained that you must talk to yourself."

I thanked him very much, and the call ended with that.

. . . Since 1971, there have been times when I faced difficult questions in life and, before I sought advice from anyone else, I would listen to my inner voice. I would set aside time to first study some of the Rebbe's teachings—like *Likutei Sichot*—in order to connect again, and then I'd follow the advice he gave me: to talk to myself. And I've encouraged other people to do the same.

Before you go asking this and that of another person, first talk to yourself and listen to what you have to say about it—sometimes your own advice is the best advice.

TEXT 13

THE REBBE, RABBI MENACHEM MENDEL SCHNEERSON,
SICHOT KODESH 5730:1, P. 361

> דער חשבון דארף זיין א חשבון צדק.
>
> ווי עס איז דא דער ווארט פון רבי'ן מהר"ש, אז "דער אויבערשטער נארט מען דאך זיכער ניט אפ חס ושלום, און די וועלט נארט מען אויך ניט אפ, נאר ער נארט זיך אליין אפ, איז דען א קונץ אז א נאר זאל אפנארן א נאר?" וואס וויבאלד אז מ'האט דאס אונז דערציילט, איז א סימן אז דאס איז אויך א נתינת כח אז דאס קען אזוי זיין.
>
> "ולא בשמים היא . . . ולא מעבר לים היא" (דברים ל, יב-יג). און ווי רש"י טייטשט, "שאילו הייתה בשמים, היית צריך לעלות אחריה וללמדה". און אויב דאס וואלט געווען "מעבר לים", וואלט מען געדארפט איבערפארן דעם ים. נאר בחסדי ה' איז דאס לא בשמים היא . . . ולא מעבר לים היא, נאר "כי קרוב אליך הדבר מאד בפיך ובלבבך", והמעשה הוא העיקר, "לעשותו" (דברים ל, יד).

We must assess ourselves honestly.

There is a saying from the fourth Lubavitcher Rebbe, Rabbi Shmuel Schneersohn, "You certainly can't mislead G-d, G-d forbid. You also can't mislead the entire world. You can only mislead yourself. So, is it an achievement to mislead a fool?" The fact that this saying was brought to our attention means that we can live up to it.

The Torah states, "It is not in the Heavens. . . . or across the ocean" (Deuteronomy 30:12–13). Rashi explains, "If it were in the Heavens, you would need to climb after it to study it." If it were across an ocean, you would need to cross the ocean. By G-d's grace, [the key to honest self-assessment] is not in the Heavens . . . or across the ocean. Rather, "It is very close to you—it is in your mouth and heart, so that you fulfill it" (Ibid., 30:14)—for action is key.

TORAH STUDIES / SEASON ONE 5785

KEY POINTS

» It is good to adopt personal stringencies and commitments for our spiritual advancement, but never at the expense of our standing obligations.

» It is good to push ourselves to be as pious, righteous, and scholarly as possible, but not at the expense of others.

» If another needs us to teach them basic Judaism, we must accept even if we had hoped to use that time for personal spiritual advancement.

» Sometimes we lack clarity on the right choice to make. However, in our heart of hearts, we always know the truth.

» To find that truth, we must consult our inner voice and assess our motives honestly.

7.
Vayishlach

Broaden Your Horizons
What an Ancient Sage's Travels Teach about Exploring New Ideas

*Dedicated in loving memory of Steven Diamond,
marking his yahrtzeit on 6 Kislev*

*May the merit of the Torah study worldwide accompany his soul
in the world of everlasting life and be a source of blessings to his
family with much health, happiness, nachas, and success.*

PARSHAH OVERVIEW

Vayishlach

Jacob returns to the Holy Land after a twenty-year stay in Charan and sends angel-emissaries to Esau in hopes of a reconciliation. But his messengers report that his brother is on the warpath with four hundred armed men. Jacob prepares for war, prays, and sends Esau a large gift (consisting of hundreds of head of livestock) to appease him.

That night, Jacob ferries his family and possessions across the Jabok River; he, however, remains behind and encounters the angel that embodies the spirit of Esau, with whom he wrestles until daybreak. Jacob suffers a dislocated hip but vanquishes the supernal creature, who bestows on him the name Israel, which means "he who prevails over the Divine."

Jacob and Esau meet, embrace, and kiss, but part ways. Jacob purchases a plot of land near Shechem, whose crown prince—also called Shechem—abducts and rapes Jacob's daughter Dinah. Dinah's brothers Simeon and Levi avenge the deed by killing all male inhabitants of the city after rendering them vulnerable by convincing them to circumcise themselves.

Jacob journeys on. Rachel dies while giving birth to her second son, Benjamin, and is buried in a roadside grave near Bethlehem. Reuben loses the birthright because he interferes with his father's marital life. Jacob arrives in Hebron to his father, Isaac, who later dies at age 180. (Rebecca had passed away before Jacob's arrival.)

Our *parshah* concludes with a detailed account of Esau's wives, children, and grandchildren; the family histories of the people of Se'ir, among whom Esau settled; and a list of the eight kings who ruled Edom, the land of Esau's and Se'ir's descendants.

INTRODUCTION

Question for Discussion

What do you enjoy most about travel?

The rules we will use to examine this Rashi are:

1. Rashi uses the explanation that is most plausible in the literal meaning of the text.

2. Rashi only includes details that are helpful to the explanation.

3. Rashi only cites the name of the sage he quotes if it contributes a key piece of understanding.

I. A HUNDRED WHAT?

The Transaction

TEXT 1A

GENESIS 33:19

> וַיִּקֶן אֶת חֶלְקַת הַשָּׂדֶה אֲשֶׁר נָטָה שָׁם אָהֳלוֹ מִיַּד בְּנֵי חֲמוֹר אֲבִי שְׁכֶם בְּמֵאָה קְשִׂיטָה.

And he purchased the part of the field where he pitched his tent from the sons of Hamor, father of Shechem, for one hundred *kesitah*.

TEXT 1B

RASHI, AD LOC.

> "קְשִׂיטָה". מָעָה. אָמַר רַבִּי עֲקִיבָא: כְּשֶׁהָלַכְתִּי לִכְרַכֵּי הַיָּם, הָיוּ קוֹרִין לְמָעָה קְשִׂיטָה.

"*Kesitah*." [A coin known as] *maah*. Rabbi Akiva said, "When I traveled to the cities by the sea, they called a *maah* "*kesitah*."

Rabbi Shlomo Yitzchaki (Rashi)
1040–1105

Most noted biblical and Talmudic commentator. Born in Troyes, France, Rashi studied in the famed *yeshivot* of Mainz and Worms. His commentaries on the Pentateuch and the Talmud, which focus on the straightforward meaning of the text, appear in virtually every edition of the Talmud and Bible.

TEXT 2A

YONATAN BEN UZIEL, *TARGUM YONATAN*, AD LOC.

> וּזְבַן יָת אַחֲסָנַת חֲקַל דִּפְרַס תַּמָּן מַשְׁכְּנֵיהּ מִן יַד בְּנֵי חֲמוֹר אָבוּי דִשְׁכֶם בְּמֵאָה מַרְגְלָיָן.

And he purchased the part of the field where he pitched his tent from the sons of Hamor, father of Shechem, for one hundred gems.

Yonatan ben Uziel
c. First Century CE

Considered by the Talmud to be Hillel the Elder's most distinguished pupil; author of the *Targum Yonatan*, also known as the Jerusalem translation, a comprehensive Aramaic translation of the Prophets. In Talmudic times, *Targum Yonatan* was read in the synagogue as a verse-by-verse translation of the Hebrew *haftorah*. Little is known about his personal life. In recent years, his tomb, in Amukah in the Galilee, has become a popular place of pilgrimage.

TEXT 2B

ONKELOS, *TARGUM ONKELOS*, AD LOC.

> וּזְבַן יָת אַחֲסָנַת חַקְלָא דִּי פְרַס תַּמָּן מַשְׁכְּנֵיהּ מִידָא דִבְנֵי חֲמוֹר אֲבוּהִי דִשְׁכֶם בְּמֵאָה חוּרְפָן.

And he purchased the part of the field where he pitched his tent from the sons of Hamor, father of Shechem, for one hundred sheep.

Onkelos
c. 35–120 CE

Famous convert to Judaism in mishnaic times. According to traditional sources, he was a prominent Roman nobleman and a nephew of the Roman emperor Titus. Author of *Targum Onkelos*, an Aramaic translation of the Bible. His *Targum* is an exposition of the interpretation of the Torah, as received by Rabbi Eliezer and Rabbi Yehoshua.

Biblical Parlance

TEXT 3A

EXODUS 30:13

> עֶשְׂרִים גֵּרָה הַשֶּׁקֶל.

A shekel is twenty *gerah*.

TEXT 3B

RASHI, AD LOC.

> "גֵּרָה". לְשׁוֹן מָעָה.

"*Gerah*." A word that means *maah*.

II. THE PRICE OF LOVE

For the Love of the Land

TEXT 4

GENESIS 33:18

> וַיָּבֹא יַעֲקֹב שָׁלֵם עִיר שְׁכֶם אֲשֶׁר בְּאֶרֶץ כְּנַעַן בְּבֹאוֹ מִפַּדַּן אֲרָם, וַיִּחַן אֶת פְּנֵי הָעִיר.

And Jacob came safely to the city of Shechem, which is in the land of Canaan, when he arrived from Padan Aram, and he encamped before the city.

TEXT 5A

MAIMONIDES, *MISHNEH TORAH*, LAWS OF KINGS AND THEIR WARS 5:10–11

> גְּדוֹלֵי הַחֲכָמִים הָיוּ מְנַשְּׁקִין עַל תְּחוּמֵי אֶרֶץ יִשְׂרָאֵל, וּמְנַשְּׁקִין אֲבָנֶיהָ, וּמִתְגַּלְגְּלִין עַל עֲפָרָהּ. וְכֵן הוּא אוֹמֵר: "כִּי רָצוּ עֲבָדֶיךָ אֶת אֲבָנֶיהָ וְאֶת עֲפָרָהּ יְחֹנֵנוּ" (תְּהִלִּים קב, טו).
>
> אָמְרוּ חֲכָמִים: כָּל הַשּׁוֹכֵן בְּאֶרֶץ יִשְׂרָאֵל עֲוֹנוֹתָיו מְחוּלִין. שֶׁנֶּאֱמַר: "וּבַל יֹאמַר שָׁכֵן חָלִיתִי הָעָם הַיּשֵׁב בָּהּ נְשֻׂא עָו‍ֹן" (יְשַׁעְיָה לג, כד).
>
> אֲפִלּוּ הָלַךְ בָּהּ אַרְבַּע אַמּוֹת, זוֹכֶה לְחַיֵּי הָעוֹלָם הַבָּא. וְכֵן הַקָּבוּר בָּהּ, נִתְכַּפֵּר לוֹ. וּכְאִלּוּ הַמָּקוֹם שֶׁהוּא בּוֹ מִזְבֵּחַ כַּפָּרָה.

Rabbi Moshe ben Maimon (Maimonides, Rambam)
1135–1204

Halachist, philosopher, author, and physician. Maimonides was born in Córdoba, Spain. After the conquest of Córdoba by the Almohads, he fled Spain and eventually settled in Cairo, Egypt. There, he became the leader of the Jewish community and served as court physician to the vizier of Egypt. He is most noted for authoring the *Mishneh Torah*, an encyclopedic arrangement of Jewish law; and for his philosophical work, *Guide for the Perplexed*. His rulings on Jewish law are integral to the formation of Halachic consensus.

Our greatest sages would kiss the borders of Israel and its stones and roll in its dust. As the Psalmist declares, "Behold, Your servants hold her stones dear and cherish her dust" (Psalms 102:15).

Our sages taught: The sins of those who dwell in Israel are forgiven, as the passage states, "The inhabitant will not say, 'I am sick'; the people who dwell there are absolved of sin" (Isaiah 33:24).

Even one who walks four cubits there will merit the World to Come. Those buried there receive atonement as if their burial place is an altar of atonement.

TEXT 5B

RABBI AVRAHAM IBN EZRA, GENESIS 33:18

> מי שיש לו בה חלק, חשוב הוא כחלק עולם הבא.

Rabbi Avraham ibn Ezra
1092–1167

Biblical commentator, linguist, and poet. Ibn Ezra was born in Toledo, Spain, and fled the Almohad regime to other parts of Europe. It is believed that he was living in London at the time of his death. Ibn Ezra is best known for his literalistic commentary on the Pentateuch. He also wrote works of poetry, philosophy, medicine, astronomy, and other topics.

Owning a portion of this Land is like owning a portion of the World to Come.

TEXT 5C

NACHMANIDES, AD LOC.

> לא רצה להיות אכסנאי בעיר, אבל רצה שתהיה תחילת ביאתו בארץ בתוך שלו, ולכן חנה בשדה וקנה המקום. וזה להחזיק בארץ.

Jacob did not want to be a guest in the city. He wanted his first entry into Israel to be on his own real estate. This is why he settled in a field and then purchased it to establish ownership in the land.

Rabbi Moshe ben Nachman (Nachmanides, Ramban)
1194–1270

Scholar, philosopher, author, and physician. Nachmanides was born in Spain and served as leader of Iberian Jewry. In 1263, he was summoned by King James of Aragon to a public disputation with Pablo Cristiani, a Jewish apostate. Though Nachmanides was the clear victor of the debate, he had to flee Spain because of the resulting persecution. He moved to Israel and helped reestablish communal life in Jerusalem. He authored a classic commentary on the Pentateuch and a commentary on the Talmud.

A Hundred Ornaments

TEXT 6

THE REBBE, RABBI MENACHEM MENDEL SCHNEERSON, *LIKUTEI SICHOT* 25, P. 182

> צו מסביר זיין וואס פאר א חשיבות קען זיין אין אזא תשלום, ברענגט
> רש"י מאמר רבי עקיבא "כשהלכתי לכרכי הים היו קורים למעה
> קשיטה"...
>
> דער וואָרט "קשיטה" [איז] פון לשון קישוטים. ווי קומט עס אז
> מ'זאל אנרופען א מעה - די קלענסטע מטבע - מיטן נאמען "קשיטה"
> (מלשון קישוטים)? זעט מען, אז ס'איז דא א פאל, אז אפילו ווען
> די שוויות פון די מטבעות מצד עצמן איז ניט גרויס, ווערן זיי אבער
> גענוצט אלס קישוטים (און זיי ווערן דערפאר אנגערופן "קשיטה").
>
> און דאס זאגט דער פסוק, אז מצד דער חיבת הארץ בעיני יעקב, האט
> ער פאר א חלקה בארץ געצאלט מיט ספעציעלע חשוב'ע מטבעות -
> "מאה קשיטה", אזעלכע מעות וואס ווערן גענוצט אלס תכשיטים.

Rabbi Menachem Mendel Schneerson
1902–1994

The towering Jewish leader of the 20th century, known as "the Lubavitcher Rebbe," or simply as "the Rebbe." Born in southern Ukraine, the Rebbe escaped Nazi-occupied Europe, arriving in the U.S. in June 1941. The Rebbe inspired and guided the revival of traditional Judaism after the European devastation, impacting virtually every Jewish community the world over. The Rebbe often emphasized that the performance of just one additional good deed could usher in the era of Mashiach. The Rebbe's scholarly talks and writings have been printed in more than 200 volumes.

To explain the significance of this coin, Rashi quotes Rabbi Akiva, "When I traveled to the cities by the sea, they called the *maah* 'kesitah.'"

The word *kesitah* connotes *kishutim*—ornaments. Why would the least valuable coin, the *maah*, be called an ornament? This demonstrates that sometimes, even if the monetary value of the coin is insignificant, it [can have sentimental value when it] is used as an adornment. They are, therefore, called ornaments.

[Using the foreign name *kesitah*] informs us that Jacob, out of love for the Land, used special coins to purchase a parcel of land in Israel, coins that doubled as ornaments.

III. NO COMPLIMENT IS NEGLIGIBLE

Rabbi Akiva

TEXT 7

TALMUD, SANHEDRIN 110B

> רבי עקיבא אומר: באים הם לעולם הבא, שנאמר: "שומר פתאים ה'" (תהלים קטז, ו).
>
> שכן קורין בכרכי הים לינוקא, פתיא.

Babylonian Talmud

A literary work of monumental proportions that draws upon the legal, spiritual, intellectual, ethical, and historical traditions of Judaism. The 37 tractates of the Babylonian Talmud contain the teachings of the Jewish sages from the period after the destruction of the 2nd Temple through the 5th century CE. It has served as the primary vehicle for the transmission of the Oral Law and the education of Jews over the centuries; it is the entry point for all subsequent legal, ethical, and theological Jewish scholarship.

Rabbi Akiva said they are granted entry into the World to Come, as the passage states, "G-d guards *peta'im*" (Psalms 116:6).

In the cities by the sea, they call a child *patya*.

TEXT 8

THE REBBE, RABBI MENACHEM MENDEL SCHNEERSON, *LIKUTEI SICHOT* 25, P. 185

> אויף אזויפיל איז געוועןן חסידותיה דרבי עקיבא צו מזכה זיין אידן, אז עס איז פאר אים געוועןן כדאי די נסיעה אין "כרכי הים", אבי צו קענען מזכה זיין את ישראל און פסק'נען אז קטני בני רשעי ישראל באים הם לעולם הבא.

So intense was Rabbi Akiva's desire to favor Jews that his entire journey to the cities by the sea would have been worthwhile merely to favor the Jews: to gain the ability to determine that children of wicked Jewish parents have a share in the World to Come, even if they die young.

TEXT 9

THE REBBE, RABBI MENACHEM MENDEL SCHNEERSON, IBID.

> און דאס איז אויך רש"י דא מרמז - "אמר רבי עקיבא כשהלכתי לכרכי הים כו'".
>
> דאס איז די זעלבע הליכה לכרכי הים ביי וועלכע רבי עקיבא האט געהערט אז "קורין לינוקא פתיא" און דערמיט האט ער ארויסגעגעבן דעם פסק לזכותם של ישראל - "קטני כו' באים הם לעולם הבא".
>
> איז ביי דער זעלבער הליכה לכרכי הים איז אויך ארויסגעקומען נאך אן ענין "רגיל לזכות", בזכותם של ישראל - די חביבות הארץ ביי יעקב'ן, אז ער האט געצאלט פאר דער חלקת השדה, וואס איז ביי אים געווען ניט מקום דירתו - "מאה קשיטה", מטבעות וואס זיינען קישוטים.

Rashi hints at this by saying, "Rabbi Akiva said, 'When I traveled to the cities by the sea . . .'"

This was the same visit to the cities by the sea during which Rabbi Akiva heard people calling children *patya*, by which he determined that children have a share in the World to Come.

This same visit to the cities by the sea yielded yet another opportunity for Rabbi Akiva, the advocate of Jews, to highlight the favor of a Jew. He discovered [an albeit minor way to demonstrate] Jacob's love of Israel. Jacob purchased land he did not intend to use as his permanent home with a hundred *kesitah*—coins that doubled as ornaments.

TEXT 10

THE REBBE, RABBI MENACHEM MENDEL SCHNEERSON, IBID., P. 184

> דערמיט איז פארשטאנדיק וואס דער פסוק איז מוסיף "במאה קשיטה".
>
> ווייל לויט שיטת רבי עקיבא - "שרגיל לזכות את ישראל" - דארף מען זוכן בא יעדער זאך, אפילו א רגיל, זכותים אויף אידן. און דערפאר, אף על פי אז דער צאלן "מאה קשיטה" איז ניט קיין געוואלדיקער חידוש, דארף מען דערציילן אויך דעם (קליינעם) זכות, מצד שהרגל נעשה טבע, צו רעדן בזכותם של ישראל.

We now understand why the Torah adds that Jacob paid a hundred *kesitah*.

According to Rabbi Akiva, who always sought to favor Jews, we must seek to highlight a Jew's strengths at every opportunity. [The Torah relates that Jacob] paid a hundred *kesitah*, though it is a minor compliment, because we must always share even minor compliments. When we get into the habit of speaking well of others, it eventually becomes [second] nature.

KEY POINTS

» Jacob loved the Holy Land so much that he insisted on purchasing even the land on which he pitched a temporary tent.

» This conveys how important it is to cultivate a love for Israel in ourselves and our children.

» Rabbi Akiva traveled and studied languages to find ways to cast Jews in the most favorable light. He used every opportunity to highlight even minor qualities of fellow Jews.

» This teaches us to look for positive qualities in the people we meet on our travels and to bring these qualities home with us to implement in our daily lives.

» It also teaches us that no compliment is negligible. Every positive quality we see in others should be highlighted.

8.
Vayeshev

Keep Climbing
Trajectory Is All That Matters

Dedicated to Mrs. Zoe Rock on the occasion of her birthday on 19 Kislev

May she go from strength to strength, along with her husband Clive and family, and enjoy good health, happiness, nachas from her loved ones, and success in all her endeavors.

PARSHAH OVERVIEW

Vayeshev

Jacob settles in Hebron with his twelve sons. His favorite is seventeen-year-old Joseph, whose brothers are jealous of the preferential treatment he receives from his father, such as a precious many-colored coat that Jacob makes for Joseph. Joseph relates to his brothers two of his dreams, which foretell that he is destined to rule over them, increasing their envy and hatred toward him.

Simeon and Levi plot to kill him, but Reuben suggests that they throw him into a pit instead, intending to come back later and save him. While Joseph is in the pit, Judah has him sold to a band of passing Ishmaelites. The brothers dip Joseph's special coat in the blood of a goat and show it to their father, leading him to believe that his most beloved son has been devoured by a wild beast.

Judah marries and has three children. The eldest, Er, dies young and childless, and his wife, Tamar, is given in levirate marriage to the second son, Onan. Onan sins by spilling his seed, and he too meets an early death. Judah is reluctant to have his third son marry her. Determined to have a child from Judah's family, Tamar disguises herself as a prostitute and seduces Judah himself. Judah hears that his daughter-in-law has become pregnant and orders her executed for harlotry, but when Tamar produces some personal effects he left with her as a pledge for payment, he publicly admits that he is the father. Tamar gives birth to twin sons, Perez (an ancestor of King David) and Zerah.

Joseph is taken to Egypt and sold to Potiphar, the minister in charge of Pharaoh's slaughterhouses. G-d blesses everything he does, and soon he is made overseer of all his master's property. Potiphar's wife desires the handsome and charismatic lad; when Joseph rejects her advances, she tells her husband that the Hebrew slave tried to force himself on her and has him thrown into prison. Joseph gains the trust and admiration of his jailers, who appoint him to a position of authority in the prison administration.

INTRODUCTION

Questions for Discussion

1. *What does being a good Jew mean to you?*
2. *Can a Jew who disregards some or all the Jewish traditions be considered a good Jew?*

The hermeneutic principles that we will employ during our examination:

1. Rashi only answers questions when they arise. He does not preview questions that will arise at a later point.
2. Rashi answers questions the first time they arise. He does not delay answering them until they arise a second time.
3. Rashi does not use extra words. If any words in his commentary appear to be extra, we misunderstood them.

I. A GEOGRAPHICAL QUESTION

A Lonely Widower

TEXT 1A

GENESIS 38:12–13

> יב. וַיִּרְבּוּ הַיָּמִים וַתָּמָת בַּת שׁוּעַ אֵשֶׁת יְהוּדָה. וַיִּנָּחֶם יְהוּדָה וַיַּעַל עַל גֹּזְזֵי צֹאנוֹ, הוּא וְחִירָה רֵעֵהוּ הָעֲדֻלָּמִי תִּמְנָתָה.
>
> יג. וַיֻּגַּד לְתָמָר לֵאמֹר, "הִנֵּה חָמִיךְ עֹלֶה תִמְנָתָה לָגֹז צֹאנוֹ".

12. And days passed and Judah's wife, the daughter of Shua, passed away. Judah was consoled and ascended with his friend, Chirah the Adullamite, to Timnah to [oversee] his sheep shearers.

13. Tamar was informed, "Behold, your father-in-law has ascended to Timnah to shear his sheep."

Where Is Timnah?

TEXT 1B

RASHI, GENESIS 38:13

> "עֹלֶה תִמְנָתָה": וּבְשִׁמְשׁוֹן הוּא אוֹמֵר, "וַיֵּרֶד שִׁמְשׁוֹן תִּמְנָתָה" (שׁוֹפְטִים יד, א). בְּשִׁפּוּעַ הָהָר הָיְתָה יוֹשֶׁבֶת, עוֹלִין לָהּ מִכָּאן וְיוֹרְדִין לָהּ מִכָּאן.

"Ascended to Timnah": But of Samson, it is written, "And Samson descended to Timnah" (Judges 14:1). The city was located on a mountain slope. One could ascend to it from the bottom and descend to it from the top.

Rabbi Shlomo Yitzchaki (Rashi)
1040–1105

Most noted biblical and Talmudic commentator. Born in Troyes, France, Rashi studied in the famed *yeshivot* of Mainz and Worms. His commentaries on the Pentateuch and the Talmud, which focus on the straightforward meaning of the text, appear in virtually every edition of the Talmud and Bible.

II. THE CITY ON THE SLOPE

Biblical Flat Talk

TEXT 2

GENESIS 22:3, 9

> וַיָּקָם וַיֵּלֶךְ אֶל הַמָּקוֹם . . . וַיָּבֹאוּ אֶל הַמָּקוֹם.

And he arose and went to the place. . . . And they came to the place.

Virtual Ascent

TEXT 3A

GENESIS 38:1

> וַיְהִי בָּעֵת הַהִיא וַיֵּרֶד יְהוּדָה מֵאֵת אֶחָיו.

And it was at that time, and Judah stepped down from among his brothers.

TEXT 3B

RASHI, AD LOC.

> שֶׁהוֹרִידוּהוּ אֶחָיו מִגְּדֻלָּתוֹ כְּשֶׁרָאוּ בְּצָרַת אֲבִיהֶם. אָמְרוּ: אַתָּה אָמַרְתָּ לְמָכְרוֹ, אִלּוּ אָמַרְתָּ לַהֲשִׁיבוֹ הָיִינוּ שׁוֹמְעִים לְךָ.

Judah's brothers demoted him from his high position when they saw their father's distress. They said, "You advised us to sell him. Had you advised us to return him, we would have obeyed you."

Physical Ascent

TEXT 4

RABBI DAVID PARDO, *MASKIL LEDAVID*, GENESIS 38:13

> דבשלמא, "ויעל" דלעיל, שפיר יש לומר דהתורה העידה "ויעל" לפי שנתעלה בה.
>
> אבל כאן דהכתוב מספר שהוגד לתמר "הנה חמיך עולה תמנתה", ליכא למימר שהמגידים לה אמרו "עולה" לפי שנתעלה בהן.

The phrase "and [he] ascended" [from verse twelve] can be interpreted as the Torah testifying that he ascended because he was elevated by his journey.

But this passage [verse thirteen], where the Torah recounts that Tamar was told, "Behold, your father-in-law has ascended to Timnah," [is different]. It cannot be said that the ordinary folk who informed her of Judah's journey used the term "ascending" because Judah would [eventually] be elevated by this journey.

Rabbi David Pardo
1718–1790

Halachic expert and liturgical poet. Rabbi Pardo served as the chief rabbi of Sarajevo, Bosnia and later moved to Jerusalem, where he headed a yeshiva and served on the rabbinic court. A prolific writer, Rabbi Pardo is best known for his multivolume commentaries on *Tosefta* and *Sifrei*, and a supercommentary to Rashi's biblical commentary.

The Slope

TEXT 5A

"FACTORS TO CONSIDER WHEN BUILDING A MOUNTAIN HOME," WWW.ZAMEEN.ORG

Enjoy stunning views of the green meadows, rugged cone-shaped mountains, woody forests, wildflowers, and clear blue skies from your living room. Living close to nature has a soothing and calming effect on your mind and soul. . . .

[Being] situated on the hillside maximizes views and natural sunlight—a prized feature that has multiple health benefits such as higher productivity, better sleep, and good mood. . . .

Tall trees, chirping birds, and fluttering butterflies are some of nature's gifts that you can enjoy at your leisure.

A mountain home is less crowded. Unlike a house in an urban setting, where you will find buzzing marketplaces and houses up close, there is peace and tranquility [when] living in a mountain home. . . .

A less crowded home means more privacy. . . . Building a house on a [mountaintop] allows you to select a location off the beaten path.

TEXT 5B

IBID.

However, bringing that picture to life is quite difficult. There are quite a few pre-construction tasks you must carry out before laying the first brick. . . .

The most challenging . . . is its foundation. Most of your budget will be spent on laying down complex foundation systems. . . . The cost of establishing the foundation layer of a mountain home is more than an entire house constructed on a flat surface.

If you have seen mudslides, you will know how important it is to have a proper solution for drainage of surface and sub-surface water when building on a mountain slope. Rainwater needs to be directed away from your home's foundation. Retaining walls must be waterproofed and drained well. There should be no water pooling near the retaining wall.

Access to the construction site is an important consideration for homeowners, contractors, and laborers. Remember to calculate the cost of transporting construction materials up the hill. The truck driver and the laborers will charge an extra amount for this.

Why on the Slope?

TEXT 6

RABBI SHMUEL EIDELS, SOTAH 10A

> דאיכא למימר דחדא כפשטיה . . . שבהר היה. ויעל כפשטיה, וירד לדרשת הגנאי.

We might suggest that there was one Timnah . . . [situated] at the top of the mountain. [Judah] ascended to it literally and [Samson] descended to it virtually.

Rabbi Shmuel Eliezer Halevi Eidels (Maharsha) 1555–1632

Rabbi, author, and Talmudist. Rabbi Eidels established a yeshiva in Posen, Poland, which was supported by his mother-in-law, Eidel (hence his surname is "Eidels"). He is primarily known for his *Chidushei Halachot,* a commentary on the Talmud in which he resolves difficulties in the texts of the Talmud, Rashi, and *Tosafot,* and which is a basic work for those who seek an in-depth understanding of the Talmud; and for his *Chidushei Agadot,* his innovative commentary on the homiletic passages of the Talmud.

The Trading Station

TEXT 7A

JERUSALEM TALMUD, SOTAH 1:8

> אמר רבי אייבו בר נגרי: כגון הדא בית מעין, שיורדין בה מפלטתה ועולין בה מטבריה.

Rabbi Ayvu son of Nagri said, "This is like Hada, the city on the spring. We descend to it from Paltata and ascend to it from Tiberias."

Jerusalem Talmud

A commentary to the Mishnah, compiled during the 4th and 5th centuries. The Jerusalem Talmud predates its Babylonian counterpart by 100 years and is written in both Hebrew and Aramaic. While the Babylonian Talmud is the most authoritative source for Jewish law, the Jerusalem Talmud remains an invaluable source for the spiritual, intellectual, ethical, historical, and legal traditions of Judaism.

TEXT 7B

THE REBBE, RABBI MENACHEM MENDEL SCHNEERSON, *LIKUTEI SICHOT* 10, P. 127

> הדוגמא מסבירה למה יצאה מהרגיל ונבנתה בשיפוע הר.
>
> כי הייתה בין שתי ערים ומובן שכל שעסקו עם שתיהן וכן בכל העסקים שבין אחת מהן עם חברתה (שצריך להיות טרדת ד"יורדין ועולין"), נוח להפגש באמצע.
>
> ואם העסקים בקביעות, בונים שם מקום קבוע (עיר).

The example explains why this city was a deviation from the norm and was built on the slope of the mountain.

Because it was between two cities, it made sense that anyone who worked with both, as well as all the business dealings between one and the other (which would require the hassle of going up and down), would conveniently meet in the middle.

If the business dealings were common, a permanent place (city) would have to be built.

Rabbi Menachem Mendel Schneerson
1902–1994

The towering Jewish leader of the 20th century, known as "the Lubavitcher Rebbe," or simply as "the Rebbe." Born in southern Ukraine, the Rebbe escaped Nazi-occupied Europe, arriving in the U.S. in June 1941. The Rebbe inspired and guided the revival of traditional Judaism after the European devastation, impacting virtually every Jewish community the world over. The Rebbe often emphasized that the performance of just one additional good deed could usher in the era of Mashiach. The Rebbe's scholarly talks and writings have been printed in more than 200 volumes.

III. KEEP CLIMBING

G-d's Mountain

TEXT 8A

PSALMS 24:3

> מִי יַעֲלֶה בְהַר ה' וּמִי יָקוּם בִּמְקוֹם קָדְשׁוֹ.

Who will climb G-d's mountain and who will arise to His holy place?

Psalms

Biblical book. The book of Psalms contains 150 psalms expressing praise for G-d, faith in G-d, and laments over tragedies. The primary author of the psalms was King David, who lived in the 9th century BCE. Psalms also contains material from earlier figures. The feelings and circumstances expressed in the psalms resonate throughout the generations, and they have become an important part of communal and personal prayer.

TEXT 8B

RABBI MENACHEM RECANATI, EXODUS 24:12

> לפי דברי רבותינו זכרונם לברכה (סוכה ה, א) נראה שלא היתה כוונתם בזאת העלייה אל ההר. שאומר שם, רבי יוסי אומר: מעולם לא ירדה שכינה למטה ולא עלה משה לרקיע . . .
>
> נראה כי כוונתם בעליית משה אל ההר, וכן עלה אל ה', אין הכוונה אל ההר, אלא ענין העלייה היא נטילת רשות לעלות ממדריגה למעלה ממדריגה.

Rabbi Menachem Recanati
c. 1250–1310

Italian rabbi and kabbalist of note. He authored *Pirush Al HaTorah*, a mystical commentary on the Bible; *Pirush Hatefilot*, a commentary on the siddur; and *Taamei Hamitzvot*, an explanation of the commandments. In addition, his Halachic rulings are collected in his *Piskei Recanati*.

From the teachings of our sages, it would appear that Moses never climbed a physical mountain. Rabbi Yossi says, "The Divine Presence never descended below, nor did Moses ascend to the Heavens" (Talmud, Sukkah 5a). . . .

I suggest that when the Torah says Moses climbed the mountain or ascended to G-d, it does not refer to an actual climb. The intention is that Moses received Divine permission to ascend to ever-higher spiritual levels.

TEXT 9

THE REBBE, RABBI MENACHEM MENDEL SCHNEERSON, *LIKUTEI SICHOT* 10, P. 127

> וידוע דכאשר האדם מטפס ועולה ההרה, אי אפשר לו להפסיק באמצע עלייתו ולעמוד זמן מה במקום שיפועו של ההר, כי כמעט מן הנמנע שלא יתמוטט ויפול למטה. אלא עליו להמשיך עלייתו בלא הפסק.
>
> וכן העניין בעליה "בהר ה'", שהתמדת העליה מוכרחת . . . בכדי להבטיח שלילת הירידה.
>
> והיינו, שאין לו להסתפק במעלתו שהגיע אליה עד כה, כי הסתפקות זו במעלתו ואי עלייתו מדרגא לדרגא במעלות הקודש, סופה שתביא לידי ירידה.

It is known that when climbing and ascending a mountain, we can't stop midway and stand for a time on the slope. If we do, it is almost inevitable that we will stumble and fall downward. Rather, we must continue our climb without pause.

Climbing G-d's mountain is similar in the sense that one must always be climbing to ensure they don't fall.

We must never be content with the spiritual level we have reached thus far. Contentment with our current level and failure to ascend from one sacred level to the next inevitably leads to descent.

LESSON 8 / KEEP CLIMBING

Timnah on the Slope

TEXT 10

THE REBBE, RABBI MENACHEM MENDEL SCHNEERSON, IBID., P. 128

> ומרומז ענין זה בדברי רש"י, שמה שנאמר לשון עליה וירידה בתמנה הוא לפי ש"בשיפוע ההר היתה יושבת".
>
> בי בשיפוע ההר (שהוא ענין העבודה להתעלות ברוחניות) נמנעת העמידה, וגם ההילוך הוא לא באופן רגיל, כי אם או עליה או ירידה.

This is implied by Rashi's words. He wrote that the reason the phrases "ascent" and "descent" apply to Timnah is because it sat "on the slope of the mountain."

The slope of the mountain, which connotes spiritual improvement, prevents one from standing still. Moreover, even ordinary walking is not possible. One can only climb, either up or down.

Conclusion

TEXT 11

RASHI, BERESHIT RABAH 85:14

> "מה פרצת עליך פרץ?"
>
> זה רבה על הפריצים. ממך יעמוד משיח, שנאמר בו: "עלה הפורץ לפניהם" (מיכה ב, יג).

"Why did you breach the breach?"

This child would be the greatest of all breachers. He would be the progenitor of the Mashiach, of whom it is written, "The breacher arose before them" (Micah 2:13).

KEY POINTS

- There are many reasons to live at the top of the mountain. Chief among them is security. There are also many difficulties in building at the mountaintop. These include grading the slope, drainage, and the cost of transporting materials and tools to the top.

- Living at the bottom of the mountain offers other benefits: ease of building, social interaction, and cultural activities.

- The hardest place to build is on the slope in the middle of the mountain. It has all the difficulties of building on a mountain, no benefits of living at the bottom, and no security that comes from living at the top.

- One reason to build on the slope is to create a trading station for cities at the top and cities at the bottom.

- Living on the slope is a metaphor for Judaism. Jewish practice is like climbing G-d's mountain. Once we embark on the climb, we must keep climbing until we reach the top. Stopping mid-climb can result in a fall. We must always see ourselves as if we are on the slope, in the middle of our climb.

APPENDIX

Avraham Fried, "Keep Climbing"

HTTPS://WWW.YOUTUBE.COM/WATCH?V=2FFZKYJAPMC

Life is a mountain we must climb
We don't have forever, just the time He gives us.
Get to the top if you can.
This is the challenge of man.

Yes, you might fall and tumble down.
Sometimes that happens when you dare.
Knowing you, my child,
You'll pick yourself up and start again from there.

Chorus
Keep climbing, don't let nothing stand in your way.
Keep believing, pay no attention to what they say.
Up is where you want to go.
It's dark and lonely down below.

Keep fighting, this is one fight you won't regret.
Keep believing, you've got what it takes now don't forget.
Up is where you belong.
It's where your soul will find her song.

Make sure you take one step at a time.
Remember that surrender is the road to no end.
Be proud of how far you've come.
You said it couldn't be done.
Dig in and breathe out there's more to climb.
To give up now would be such an awful shame.
Give it all you've got, my child.
You don't want to lose all that you have gained.

(Chorus)

There's no thrill when standing still.
But there is a way when there is a will.
Touch the Divine!
Continue to climb!

(Chorus)

Life is a mountain we must climb

9.
Chanukah

"Take the First Step. I'll Do the Rest."
One Small Step from Man, One Giant Step from G-d

Dedicated in loving memory of Sala and Jack Tellerman

May the merit of the Torah study worldwide accompany their souls in the world of everlasting life and be a source of blessings to their family with much health, happiness, nachas, and success

HOLIDAY OVERVIEW

Chanukah

Chanukah—the eight-day Festival of Lights that begins on the eve of the twenty-fifth day of the Jewish month of Kislev—celebrates the triumph of light over darkness, of purity over adulteration, and of spirituality over materialism.

More than twenty-one centuries ago, the Holy Land was ruled by the Seleucids (Syrian-Greeks), who sought to forcefully Hellenize the people of Israel. Against all odds, a small band of faithful Jews defeated one of the mightiest armies on earth, drove the Greeks from the Land, reclaimed the Holy Temple in Jerusalem, and rededicated it to the service of G-d.

When they sought to light the Temple's *menorah* (the seven-branched candelabrum), they found only a single cruse of olive oil that had escaped contamination by the Greeks; miraculously, the one-day supply burned for eight days, until new oil could be prepared under conditions of ritual purity.

To commemorate and publicize these miracles, the sages instituted the festival of Chanukah. At the heart of the festival is the nightly menorah (candelabrum) lighting: a single flame on the first night, two on the second evening, and so on till the eighth night of Chanukah, when all eight lights are kindled.

On Chanukah, we also add Hallel and *ve'al hanisim* in our daily prayers to offer praise and thanksgiving to G-d for "delivering the strong into the hands of the weak, the many into the hands of the few, . . . the wicked into the hands of the righteous."

Chanukah customs include eating foods fried in oil—latkes (potato pancakes) and *sufganiyot* (doughnuts)—playing with the dreidel (a spinning top on which are inscribed the Hebrew letters *nun*, *gimel*, *hei,* and *shin*—an acronym for "*nes gadol hayah sham*—a great miracle happened there"), and the giving of Chanukah *gelt*—gifts of money—to children.

INTRODUCTION

Question for Discussion

If G-d intended to save the Jews miraculously, why did He force them to fight a war, scrounge about for oil, and kindle the candelabra every night? He could have just stepped in and saved them. He could have popped oil into the candelabra and made it burn without any effort from our ancestors.

> Here is a list of rules that we will use to examine this Rashi:
>
> 1. Rashi always chooses the simplest explanation supported by a literal reading of the text.
> 2. Rashi only brings two explanations when something is missing from each.
> 3. Rashi only cites the source if necessary to help us understand his explanation.
> 4. If you dig deep into Rashi's words, you will find deep mystical teachings called the "wine" of the Torah.

I. WHO BUILT IT?

The Candelabra

TEXT 1A

NUMBERS 8:4

> וְזֶה מַעֲשֵׂה הַמְּנֹרָה מִקְשָׁה זָהָב, עַד יְרֵכָהּ עַד פִּרְחָהּ מִקְשָׁה הִיא, כַּמַּרְאֶה אֲשֶׁר הֶרְאָה ה' אֶת מֹשֶׁה כֵּן עָשָׂה אֶת הַמְּנֹרָה.

This is the work of the candelabra hammered from gold; from its base to its flower, it was hammered; according to the image that G-d showed Moses, so did he construct the candelabra.

TEXT 1B

RASHI, AD LOC.

> מִי שֶׁעֲשָׂאָהּ.
> וּמִדְרַשׁ אַגָּדָה, עַל יְדֵי הַקָּדוֹשׁ בָּרוּךְ הוּא נַעֲשֵׂית מֵאֵלֶיהָ.

The one who made it [whomever it may have been].

The Midrash suggests it was made by itself through the hands of G-d.

Rabbi Shlomo Yitzchaki (Rashi)
1040–1105

Most noted biblical and Talmudic commentator. Born in Troyes, France, Rashi studied in the famed *yeshivot* of Mainz and Worms. His commentaries on the Pentateuch and the Talmud, which focus on the straightforward meaning of the text, appear in virtually every edition of the Talmud and Bible.

Unusual Answers

TEXT 2

RASHI, GENESIS 41:13

> וְכֵן דֶּרֶךְ כָּל מִקְרָאוֹת קְצָרִים . . . הֵם סוֹתְמִים אֶת הַדָּבָר.

This is common for all cryptic passages. . . . They leave the matter unspecified.

II. A SPECIAL DESIGN

The Repetition

TEXT 3

RASHI, NUMBERS 8:2

> שֶׁכְּשֶׁרָאָה אַהֲרֹן חֲנֻכַּת הַנְּשִׂיאִים חָלְשָׁה אָז דַּעְתּוֹ, שֶׁלֹּא הָיָה עִמָּהֶם בַּחֲנֻכָּה לֹא הוּא וְלֹא שִׁבְטוֹ.
>
> אָמַר לוֹ הַקָּדוֹשׁ בָּרוּךְ הוּא: חַיֶּיךָ, שֶׁלְּךָ גְדוֹלָה מִשֶּׁלָּהֶם, שֶׁאַתָּה מַדְלִיק וּמֵטִיב אֶת הַנֵּרוֹת.

When Aaron saw the inaugural offerings of the tribal princes, he was distressed over not joining them personally or on behalf of his tribe.

G-d, therefore, said to him, "By your life, your honor is greater than theirs, for you will kindle and prepare the lights."

A Special Design

TEXT 4

RASHI, EXODUS 25:40

> שֶׁנִּתְקַשָּׁה מֹשֶׁה בְּמַעֲשֵׂה הַמְּנוֹרָה, עַד שֶׁהֶרְאָה לוֹ הַקָּדוֹשׁ בָּרוּךְ הוּא מְנוֹרָה שֶׁל אֵשׁ.

Moses had difficulty understanding how to make the candelabra until G-d showed him the candelabra in an image of fire.

TEXT 5

TALMUD, SHABBAT 22B

> וכי לאורה הוא צריך? והלא כל ארבעים שנה שהלכו בני ישראל במדבר לא הלכו אלא לאורו?
>
> אלא עדות היא לבאי עולם שהשכינה שורה בישראל.
>
> מאי עדות?
>
> אמר רב: זו נר מערבי. שנותן בה שמן כמדת חברותיה, וממנה היה מדליק ובה היה מסיים.

Does G-d require the light of the candelabra? Was it not G-d who lit the path for the Jews for forty years as they traveled [at night] across the desert?

Rather, the lights of the candelabra testify to the entire world that the Divine Presence dwells among the Jews.

What is the nature of this testimony?

Rav explained, "It is the westernmost lamp. It was filled with the same measure of oil as the other lamps, yet the other lamps were kindled from its light, and it was the last to be kindled."

Babylonian Talmud

A literary work of monumental proportions that draws upon the legal, spiritual, intellectual, ethical, and historical traditions of Judaism. The 37 tractates of the Babylonian Talmud contain the teachings of the Jewish sages from the period after the destruction of the 2nd Temple through the 5th century CE. It has served as the primary vehicle for the transmission of the Oral Law and the education of Jews over the centuries; it is the entry point for all subsequent legal, ethical, and theological Jewish scholarship.

The Anonymous Artisan

TEXT 6A

THE REBBE, RABBI MENACHEM MENDEL SCHNEERSON, *LIKUTEI SICHOT* 38, P. 36

> ולכן מפרש רש"י, "כן עשה את המנורה - מי שעשאה".
>
> היינו שבדיוק ובכוונה לא פירש הכתוב מיהו העושה, כי אין כוונת הכתוב לספר בשבחו של האדם העושה, אלא לבאר מעלת המנורה (ללא נפקא מינה מיהו העושה), שעשיית המנורה... היתה "כמראה אשר הראה ה' את משה".

Rashi's [first] explanation is, "The one who made it [whomever it may have been]."

The Torah deliberately conceals the constructor's identity because the Torah's intention is not to praise the artisan who constructed it [for not deviating from G-d's instructions]. The Torah intends to demonstrate the importance of the candelabra regardless of who made it. It is important because it was made according to an image shown by G-d to Moses.

Rabbi Menachem Mendel Schneerson 1902–1994

The towering Jewish leader of the 20th century, known as "the Lubavitcher Rebbe," or simply as "the Rebbe." Born in southern Ukraine, the Rebbe escaped Nazi-occupied Europe, arriving in the U.S. in June 1941. The Rebbe inspired and guided the revival of traditional Judaism after the European devastation, impacting virtually every Jewish community the world over. The Rebbe often emphasized that the performance of just one additional good deed could usher in the era of Mashiach. The Rebbe's scholarly talks and writings have been printed in more than 200 volumes.

G-d Did It

TEXT 6B

THE REBBE, RABBI MENACHEM MENDEL SCHNEERSON, IBID., PP. 36–37

> על פי זה מתיישב היטב הטעם שלא הסתפק רש"י בפירוש הא' אלא הביא גם פירוש ה"מדרש אגדה" ש"על ידי הקדוש ברוך הוא נעשית מאליה".
>
> כי לפירוש זה מבוארת עוד יותר מעלתה של המנורה מכל כלי המשכן, שלא רק שנעשית על פי ה"מראה אשר הראה ה' את משה", אלא עוד זאת, שגם עשייתה בפועל היתה על ידי הקדוש ברוך הוא.
>
> ונמצא, שאהרן זכה לחנך כלי שהיה מעשה ידי הקדוש ברוך הוא.

This explains why Rashi was not content with his first explanation and added the Midrashic explanation that the candelabra was made by itself through the hands of G-d.

This Midrash further underscores the uniqueness of the candelabra among the Tabernacle's artifacts. It was not only made according to an image that G-d showed Moses, but moreover, it was constructed by G-d's hands.

Aaron had the greatest privilege of all: to inaugurate an artifact constructed by G-d.

III. THE CELESTIAL-TERRESTRIAL PARTNERSHIP

Did G-d Change His Mind?

TEXT 7A

RABBI YEHUDAH LOEW, *GUR ARYEH*, NUMBERS 8:4

> ודאי אי אפשר לומר שהיתה המנורה נעשית לגמרי מאליה, שהרי המנורה מצוה על ישראל לעשות... "ועשית מנורת זהב" (שמות כה, לא), שתראה מזה שהיתה המצוה על ישראל לעשות המנורה. ואין לומר כלל שיהיו ישראל חסרים מצוה אחת.
>
> אלא כך הפירוש, כי השליך הככר לאור, והיתה נעשה המנורה באש כשהיה משה מכה בפטיש עליה, ונעשה הכל. ואם לא היה יודע משה רבינו צורת המנורה, איך יעשה. אבל ידע באיזה מקום הגביעים והכפתורים והפרחים, ושם היה מכה ונעשה מאליה.

Rabbi Yehudah Loew (Maharal of Prague) 1525–1609

Talmudist and philosopher. Maharal rose to prominence as leader of the famed Jewish community of Prague. He is the author of more than a dozen works of original philosophic thought, including *Tiferet Yisrael* and *Netzach Yisrael*. He also authored *Gur Aryeh*, a supercommentary to Rashi's biblical commentary; and a commentary on the nonlegal passages of the Talmud. He is buried in the Old Jewish Cemetery of Prague.

It is impossible to suggest that the candelabra was made entirely by itself if G-d said, . . . "And you should make a candelabra of gold" (Exodus 25:31). G-d instructed that it be constructed by the Israelites, and we cannot suggest that the Jews failed to obey one of G-d's commandments.

Rather, this is how the candelabra came to be. Moses threw a slab of gold into the flame, and as he hammered at it, the candelabra made itself. Moses knew the design; otherwise, he would not know where and how to hammer. So, he hammered in the appropriate spots for the cups, buttons, and flowers, and the candelabra emerged by itself [through the hands of G-d].

Why the Mortal?

TEXT 7B

RABBI YEHUDAH LOEW, IBID.

> וכך הוא כל מעשה שפועל ה', הכל צריך פועל למטה. וה' יתברך גומר על ידו.
>
> שהרי קריעת ים סוף, שהקדוש ברוך הוא עשה. ואפילו הכי הוצרך משה לעשות פעל למטה, כדכתיב: (שמות יד, טז) "ואתה הרם ידך ובקעהו". שה' יתברך גומר על ידי אדם, ודבר זה ברור.
>
> ולפיכך היה צריך משה לדעת כל מעשה המנורה, והיה פועל כפי מה שהיה יכול, והקדוש ברוך הוא גומר על ידו.

Every miraculous intervention is initiated by mortal effort. We begin the effort, and G-d intervenes to conclude it.

Take, for example, the Splitting of the Sea of Reeds: It was a Divine miracle, but with an effort by Moses, as the passage states, "And you raise your arm and split it" (Exodus 14:16). It is clear that G-d only completes what we mortals initiate.

This is why Moses needed to master the complex design of the candelabra and construct as much as he could. Only then would G-d complete what Moses began.

Not Just Moses

TEXT 8

TALMUD, SOTAH 37A

> קפץ נחשון בן עמינדב וירד לים תחילה . . . ועליו מפרש בקבלה: "הושיעני אלקים כי באו מים עד נפש, טבעתי ביון מצולה ואין מעמד וגו'" (תהלים סט, ב). "אל תשטפני שבולת מים ואל תבלעני מצולה וגו'" (תהלים סט, טז).
>
> באותה שעה היה משה מאריך בתפלה. אמר לו הקדוש ברוך הוא: ידידיי טובעים בים, ואתה מאריך בתפלה לפני?
>
> אמר לפניו: רבונו של עולם, ומה בידי לעשות?
>
> אמר לו: "דבר אל בני ישראל ויסעו, ואתה הרם את מטך ונטה את ידך וגו'" (שמות יד, טו-טז).

Nahshon the son of Amminadab was the first to jump and descend into the sea. . . . It was with regard to Nahshon that the psalmist wrote, "Save me, G-d, for the waters threaten my life; I have sunk in muddy depths, and there is no place to stand" (Psalms 69:2–3) and "May the currents not sweep me away, nor the deep swallow me" (Psalms 69:16).

At that moment, Moses was deeply immersed in prayer. G-d said to him, "My loved ones are drowning in the sea, and you stand before Me immersed in prayer?"

Moses replied, "Master of the universe, what can I possibly do?"

G-d replied, "Tell the Children of Israel to journey forth. And you raise your staff and stretch your hand over the sea" (Exodus 14:15–16).

KEY POINTS

» Aaron was disappointed to have been left out of the offerings that inaugurated the altar. G-d offered something better: to inaugurate the candelabra.

» Rashi suggests two reasons the candelabra was better than the altar: (1) it was the only artifact made according to an image that G-d showed Moses, and (2) it was made by G-d.

» The purpose of the candelabra was not to light up the Temple but to spread G-d's light to the world.

» Moses struggled to construct a material artifact channeling G-d's light. So G-d made it instead.

» Nevertheless, G-d told Moses to make as much of the candelabra as a mortal could, and G-d would do the rest. G-d wants His miracles to be a partnership. We initiate the effort, and He takes over and completes the task. When we invest in the miracle, it has an indelible impact on us.

10.
Vayigash

When You're in Pain, Start Yelling
Standing Up for Your Beliefs

*Dedicated to Francine Gani, in appreciation for her friendship
and partnership with JLI, and her dedication to bringing
the light of Torah to communities across the globe*

PARSHAH OVERVIEW

Vayigash

Judah approaches Joseph to plead for the release of Benjamin, offering himself as a slave to the Egyptian ruler in Benjamin's stead. Upon witnessing his brothers' loyalty to one another, Joseph reveals his identity to them. "I am Joseph," he declares. "Is my father still alive?"

The brothers are overcome by shame and remorse, but Joseph comforts them. "It was not you who sent me here," he says to them, "but G-d. It has all been ordained from Above to save us, and the entire region, from famine."

The brothers rush back to Canaan with the news. Jacob comes to Egypt with his sons and their families—seventy souls in all—and is reunited with his beloved son after twenty-two years. On his way to Egypt he receives the Divine promise: "Fear not to go down to Egypt, for I will there make of you a great nation. I will go down with you into Egypt, and I will also surely bring you up again."

Joseph gathers the wealth of Egypt by selling food and seed during the famine. Pharaoh gives Jacob's family the fertile country of Goshen to settle, and the Children of Israel prosper in their Egyptian exile.

INTRODUCTION

The rules we will use to analyze Rashi's comment:

1. If an unusual expression, or a word that requires translation, appears in the Torah more than once, Rashi will explain it the first time it appears. After that, Rashi assumes that we know its meaning each time it appears.

2. In his header, Rashi always quotes the words from the passage he intends to explain. If he quotes words he doesn't explain, it must be that they contribute to, prove, or support the explanation that's about to come.

I. AN ODD PHRASE

Judah Confronts Joseph

TEXT 1A

GENESIS 44:18

> וַיִּגַּשׁ אֵלָיו יְהוּדָה וַיֹּאמֶר בִּי אֲדֹנִי, יְדַבֶּר נָא עַבְדְּךָ דָבָר בְּאָזְנֵי אֲדֹנִי וְאַל יִחַר אַפְּךָ בְּעַבְדֶּךָ, כִּי כָמוֹךָ כְּפַרְעֹה.

And Judah approached Joseph and said, "Please, my master, allow your servant to speak a matter into my master's ears, and let your wrath not be kindled against your servant, for you are like Pharaoh."

TEXT 1B

RASHI, AD LOC.

> "וַיִּגַּשׁ אֵלָיו . . . דָבָר בְּאָזְנֵי אֲדֹנִי". יִכָּנְסוּ דְבָרַי בְּאָזְנֶיךָ.

"And Judah approached Joseph . . . 'a matter into my master's ears.'" May my words enter your ears.

Rabbi Shlomo Yitzchaki (Rashi)
1040–1105

Most noted biblical and Talmudic commentator. Born in Troyes, France, Rashi studied in the famed *yeshivot* of Mainz and Worms. His commentaries on the Pentateuch and the Talmud, which focus on the straightforward meaning of the text, appear in virtually every edition of the Talmud and Bible.

For the Fifth Time

TEXT 2A

GENESIS 20:8

> וַיַּשְׁכֵּם אֲבִימֶלֶךְ בַּבֹּקֶר וַיִּקְרָא לְכָל עֲבָדָיו, וַיְדַבֵּר אֶת כָּל הַדְּבָרִים הָאֵלֶּה בְּאָזְנֵיהֶם.

And Abimelech arose early in the morning, and summoned all his servants, and spoke all these words into their ears.

TEXT 2B

GENESIS 23:13

> וַיְדַבֵּר אֶל עֶפְרוֹן בְּאָזְנֵי עַם הָאָרֶץ.

And he spoke to Efron into the ears of the people of the land.

II. LISTEN WHEN I SCREAM

A Matter of Context

TEXT 3

RABBI CHAIM IBN ATAR, *OR HACHAYIM* 44:18

> צריך לדעת, למה הוצרך לומר "ויגש", אחר שקרוב אליו היה ומדבר עמו עד עתה? . . .
>
> אכן פשט הכתוב הוא, כי דבר ידוע הוא כי מנהג המלכים ישבו לפניהם גדולי המלכיות ושריהם ויועציהם. והיה אם בא איש על דבר משפט או דבר מאת המלך, לא יעמוד בהפסק בין המלך ושריו היושבים ראשונה במלכות, וחוץ לעגול יעמוד ושם ידבר.
>
> וכמו כן היה מדבר יהודה עד עתה, ואחר כך "ויגש אליו", פירוש שנכנס לפנים ממחיצתו ועמד בין המלך ובין השרים, כדי שלא ישמעו דבריו לזולת המלך.

Rabbi Chaim ibn Atar (*Or Hachayim*)
1696–1743

Biblical exegete, kabbalist, and Talmudist. Rabbi Atar, born in Meknes, Morocco, was a prominent member of the Moroccan rabbinate and later immigrated to the Land of Israel. He is most famous for his *Or Hachayim*, a popular commentary on the Torah. The famed Jewish historian and bibliophile Rabbi Chaim Yosef David Azulai was among his most notable disciples.

We need to clarify: Why does the Torah tell us that Judah approached Joseph if he was already in close proximity to him, considering that they had already been conversing? . . .

It is well known that kings are customarily accompanied by their high-ranking courtiers, ministers, and advisors. When people are granted an audience with the king, they are not invited to advance past the high-ranking ministers and stand directly before the king. Rather, they stand beyond the circle of royal advisors and address the king from there.

This is how Judah addressed Joseph until this point. Then he approached Joseph, meaning he stepped past his station and stood between the king and his ministers so that only the king would hear his words.

Pay Close Attention to Some Straight Talk

TEXT 4

RABBI YOSEF YITZCHAK SCHNEERSOHN, *SEFER HAMAAMARIM* 5708, P. 252

> וואס מען מיינט "דערהערן", ווייס א חסידישער איד זייער גוט. מען האט שוין אמאל גערעדט בארוכה דעם חילוק פון "הערן" ביז "דערהערן".
>
> "הערן" מיינט מען אויך ניט סתם הערן מיט די כלי השמיעה אליין. סתם הערן מיט די כלי השמיעה הייסט נאך ניט געהערט, דאס איז נאר אין איין אויער אריין און פון דעם צווייטן ארוים.
>
> "הערן" מיינט מען על דרך ווי עס שטייט: "דבר כי שומע עבדיך" (שמואל א ג, י). וואס דער פירוש פון "שומע" מיינט מען פארשטיין. די קאפ הערט, דאס הייסט, די פארשטאנד הערט. וואס אויף דעם שטייט: "אזן מלין תבחן" (איוב יב, א), מען פארשטייט דאס וואס מען הערט.
>
> "דערהערן" איז גאר עטוואס אנדערש, ווען דער אזן שומעת פירט אריין דעם דערהער אין אלע איברים ממש.

Rabbi Yosef Yitzchak Schneersohn
(Rayatz, Frierdiker Rebbe, Previous Rebbe)
1880–1950

Chasidic rebbe, prolific writer, and Jewish activist. Rabbi Yosef Yitzchak, the 6th leader of the Chabad movement, actively promoted Jewish religious practice in Soviet Russia and was arrested for these activities. After his release from prison and exile, he settled in Warsaw, Poland, from where he fled Nazi occupation and arrived in New York in 1940. Settling in Brooklyn, Rabbi Schneersohn worked to revitalize American Jewish life. His son-in-law Rabbi Menachem Mendel Schneerson succeeded him as the leader of the Chabad movement.

A Chasid is very familiar with what we mean when we say *derheren*. We once discussed the difference between *heren* and *derheren* at length.

Heren doesn't mean listening only with one's ears. Listening with one's ears is not really listening. It goes in one ear and out the other.

Heren is like the phrase, "Speak, for your servant is listening" (1 Samuel 3:10). The meaning of listening is to understand. The brain listens, the intellect listens. It is like the phrase, "The ear examines words" (Job 12:11). To understand what we hear.

Derheren is very different. It is when the listening ear carries the insight to literally every organ in the body.

LESSON 10 / WHEN YOU'RE IN PAIN, START YELLING

TEXT 5

RASHI, GENESIS 44:18

> "וְאַל יִחַר אַפְּךָ". מִכָּאן אַתָּה לָמֵד שֶׁדִּבֵּר אֵלָיו קָשׁוֹת.

"Let your wrath not be kindled." From here we discern that Judah spoke forcefully to Joseph.

III. EXISTENTIAL CONCERNS

As Important as Ice Cream

Question for Discussion

What is the difference between the way three-year-olds ask for ice cream and adults ask for a raise?

TEXT 6

THE REBBE, RABBI MENACHEM MENDEL SCHNEERSON, *LIKUTEI SICHOT* 20, P. 216

> כל זמן עס האנדלט זיך וועגן עניינים חצוניים, געלט-פארדינסטן וכדומה, פירט מען זיך לויט שכל'דיקע חשבונות און מ'רעכנט אויס ווי עס לוינט זיך בעסער.
>
> בשעת אבער עס קומט צו אן עניין פון "ונפשו קשורה בנפשו" (בראשית מד, ל), אן עניין וואס רירט אן בנפשו של בנימין ובנפשו של יעקב, דאן מאכט מען ניט קיין חשבונות ווי עס לוינט זיך בעסער און מען הויבט אן גלייך מיטן גאנצן שטורעם, וכמאמר העולם: אז עס טוט-וויי, שרייט מען.

Rabbi Menachem Mendel Schneerson
1902–1994

The towering Jewish leader of the 20th century, known as "the Lubavitcher Rebbe," or simply as "the Rebbe." Born in southern Ukraine, the Rebbe escaped Nazi-occupied Europe, arriving in the U.S. in June 1941. The Rebbe inspired and guided the revival of traditional Judaism after the European devastation, impacting virtually every Jewish community the world over. The Rebbe often emphasized that the performance of just one additional good deed could usher in the era of Mashiach. The Rebbe's scholarly talks and writings have been printed in more than 200 volumes.

So long as we are dealing with shallow concerns, monetary profits and the like, we approach the matter rationally and determine the most effective way to address it.

When we deal with a matter of "his soul is tied to his soul" (Genesis 44:30), something that endangers the lives of Benjamin and [his aged father] Jacob, we don't make rational determinations about the best approach. We begin by making a tumult. As the saying goes, one screams when it hurts.

LESSON 10 / WHEN YOU'RE IN PAIN, START YELLING

TEXT 7

THE REBBE, RABBI MENACHEM MENDEL SCHNEERSON, IBID., P. 217

> אין די זאכן איז אדרבה, דברי קשות איבערצייגן דעם הערער אז דאס
> איז באמת נוגע, נוגע בנפש. ניט ער מיינט געלט, א ביינקל, כבוד,
> וכיוצא בזה.
>
> דאס מאכט אז "יכנסו דברי באזניך": ער הויבט אן גלייך מיט א
> שטורעם, ער "קלאפט אויפן טיש", און רעכנט זיך ניט מיט קיין
> דיפלאמאטישע חשבונות, דערפילט דער צווייטער ווי די זאך איז
> דעם מדבר נוגע אין פנימיות הנפש. ווירקט עס אויפן צווייטן ער זאל
> זיך אונטערגעבן און נאכגעבן, ביז אס עס ווערט בנחת וברצון.

In these matters, strong words convince the listener that the matter is truly existential. We are not concerned with money, prestige, power, and the like.

This approach results in "may my words enter your ears." When we begin with a tumult, bang on the table, and eschew diplomatic niceties, others realize that this is truly an existential matter for us. This convinces them to concede and grant our demands. Eventually, they [come around to our perspective and] grant it happily and willingly.

In Israel

TEXT 8

THE REBBE, RABBI MENACHEM MENDEL SCHNEERSON, "THE REBBE ON HOW TO HANDLE A U.S. SECRETARY OF STATE," WWW.YOUTUBE.COM

The solution to these unpleasant situations is the opposite of what was done until now. Up to now, the approach has been to compromise on vital issues, not just minor ones, to receive something in return. . . . We opened negotiations by insisting that [the subject at hand] is a matter of survival, but since we are alone among "seventy nations," we feel we have no choice but to compromise. The problem is that once we make concessions, it is impossible to find the point at which compromises must end.

. . . The only approach that has worked with the United States until now has been to stand firmly and explain that it is not about stubbornness, but a matter of survival.

Communicating with Our Children

TEXT 9

THE REBBE, RABBI MENACHEM MENDEL SCHNEERSON, *LIKUTEI SICHOT* 20, P. 217

> מען דארף גלייך בזריזות הכי גדולה אנהויבן מיטן גרעסטן שטורעם אויף מציל זיין דעם קינד פון חינוך והנהגת מצרים, חינוך היפך התורה, וועלכער פירט צו התבוללות – פקוח נפשות ממש.
>
> און בשעת מען גייט מיט דער וועג, דערפירט עס צו דעם, אזוי ווי ס'איז געוווען בא "ויגש אליו יהודה" (בראשית מד, יח), אז דורך דעם וואס יהודה איז ארויסגעקומען מיט א שטורעם איז ניט נאר עס איז ניט געוווען דער ענין פון "עבדים" און עבדות, נאר אדרבה - "ויאמר פרעה גו' ואתנה לכם את טוב ארץ מצרים" (בראשית מה, יז-יח), און נאך פאר דעם, "לפניו" - מאכט מען "בית תלמוד שמשם תצא הוראה" אין מצרים.
>
> מען איז מחנך אז די תלמידים וויסן קלאר ווי בני יעקב דארפן זיך אויפפירן און וויסן און קענען זיין בעלי הוראה.

We must make an immediate tumult, and with great alacrity, to save our children from an education and behaviors that were prevalent in Egypt: an education that is opposite to that of the Torah—one that leads to assimilation, which imperils their spiritual life.

This approach yields the results that were achieved when "Judah approached Joseph" (Genesis 44:18). Because Judah began by making a tumult, Jacob's family did not suffer slavery [until much later]. On the contrary, "Pharaoh said, . . . 'I will give you the best of the land of Egypt'" (Genesis 45:17–18). Even before Jacob's family arrived in Egypt, [Judah went ahead and] established a Talmudic academy in Egypt, where Halachic rulings were formulated.

This means that we educate our children to know precisely how descendants of Jacob are meant to behave and even to become authorities on Jewish law.

KEY POINTS

» Judah was about to talk forcefully to Joseph, in a manner unbecoming toward a royal. Out of respect for Joseph, he did not want others to overhear. He therefore walked up to him and spoke quietly.

» Though he was about to speak forcefully, he wanted Joseph to listen with an open mind and heart. He therefore prefaced his remarks with a plea that his words enter into Joseph's ears.

» When we discuss matters that are not existential, it is important to talk diplomatically and show respect for both sides.

» When we discuss matters of existential importance, we must state our views forcefully so that others realize that there is no room for negotiation: that it is a matter of critical importance.

» At the same time, our tone must be respectful and loving. We want to be on the offense, but we don't want to be offensive. This gives the other person the best chance of accepting our message.

11.
Vayechi

You Can Clean Up Your Own Mess
No Mistake Is Too Great to Fix

Dedicated to Dr. Lana and Howard Tiersky, in appreciation for their friendship and partnership with JLI and The Wellness Institute, and their dedication to bringing the light of Torah to communities across the globe.

PARSHAH OVERVIEW
Vayechi

Jacob lives the final seventeen years of his life in Egypt. Before his passing, he asks Joseph to take an oath that he will bury him in the Holy Land. He blesses Joseph's two sons, Manasseh and Ephraim, elevating them to the status of his own sons as progenitors of tribes within the nation of Israel.

The patriarch desires to reveal the end of days to his children but is prevented from doing so.

Jacob blesses his sons, assigning to each his role as a tribe: Judah will produce leaders, legislators, and kings; priests will come from Levi; scholars from Issachar; seafarers from Zebulun; schoolteachers from Simeon; soldiers from Gad; judges from Dan; olive growers from Asher; and so on. Reuben is rebuked for "confusing his father's marriage bed"; Simeon and Levi, for the massacre of Shechem and the plot against Joseph. Naphtali is granted the swiftness of a deer; Benjamin, the ferociousness of a wolf; and Joseph is blessed with beauty and fertility.

A large funeral procession, consisting of Jacob's descendants, Pharaoh's ministers, the leading citizens of Egypt, and the Egyptian cavalry accompanies Jacob on his final journey to the Holy Land, where he is buried in the Machpelah Cave in Hebron.

Joseph, too, dies in Egypt, at the age of 110. He, too, instructs that his bones be taken out of Egypt and buried in the Holy Land, but this would come to pass only with the Israelites' Exodus from Egypt many years later. Before his passing, Joseph conveys to the Children of Israel the testament from which they will draw their hope and faith in the difficult years to come: "G-d will surely remember you and bring you up out of this land to the land that He swore to Abraham, Isaac, and Jacob."

INTRODUCTION

Question for Discussion

What would you do?

A. *Take care of yourself.*

B. *Help as many people as reasonably possible.*

C. *Take charge of the neighborhood, though you have no idea where to begin and what to do.*

The hermeneutic rules we will employ while examining this Rashi:

1. Rashi does not use extra words. If extra words seem to appear in his writing, they are not superfluous; they are highly instructive.

2. Rashi uses explanations that make the most sense in the plain meaning of the text. If Rashi opts for an explanation that seems overly sophisticated, we did not understand his intent.

3. If Rashi disregards a reason brought by other commentaries, there must be a reason for it.

I. THE BLESSING

A Plucky Wolf

TEXT 1

GENESIS 49:27

> בִּנְיָמִין זְאֵב יִטְרָף בַּבֹּקֶר יֹאכַל עַד וְלָעֶרֶב יְחַלֵּק שָׁלָל.

Benjamin, a preying wolf; in the morning he will devour plunder, and in the evening, he will divide the spoils.

TEXT 2A

MIDRASH, *BERESHIT RABAH* 49:3

> שָׁאוּל אֶת הַמְּלוּכָה, שֶׁנֶּאֱמַר: "וְשָׁאוּל לָכַד אֶת הַמְּלוּכָה עַל יִשְׂרָאֵל" (שְׁמוּאֵל א יד, מז).

Saul [plucked] the kingdom, as the passage states, "Saul captured the kingdom" (1 Samuel 14:47).

Bereshit Rabah

An early rabbinic commentary on the Book of Genesis. This Midrash bears the name of Rabbi Oshiyah Rabah (Rabbi Oshiya "the Great"), whose teaching opens this work. This Midrash provides textual exegeses and stories, expounds upon the biblical narrative, and develops and illustrates moral principles. Produced by the sages of the Talmud in the Land of Israel, its use of Aramaic closely resembles that of the Jerusalem Talmud. It was first printed in Constantinople in 1512 together with 4 other Midrashic works on the other 4 books of the Pentateuch.

TEXT 2B

MIDRASH, *BERESHIT RABAH* 49:3

> רַבִּי פִּינְחָס פָּתַר קַרְיָא בַּמִּזְבֵּחַ. מַה הַזְּאֵב הַזֶּה חוֹטֵף, כָּךְ הָיָה הַמִּזְבֵּחַ חוֹטֵף אֶת הַקָּרְבָּנוֹת.

Rabbi Pinchas applied the blessing to the altar [in the Temple]. As a wolf snatches its prey, so did the altar snatch the offerings.

Rashi's Explanation

TEXT 2C

RASHI, GENESIS 49:27

> "בִּנְיָמִין זְאֵב יִטְרָף": זְאֵב הוּא אֲשֶׁר יִטְרָף. נִבָּא עַל שֶׁיִּהְיוּ עֲתִידִין לִהְיוֹת חַטְפָנִין, "וַחֲטַפְתֶּם לָכֶם אִישׁ אִשְׁתּוֹ" (שׁוֹפְטִים כא, כא), בְּפִלֶגֶשׁ בַּגִּבְעָה.

"Benjamin, a preying wolf": Jacob prophesied that the tribe of Benjamin would become snatchers, as the verse states, "And each man must snatch his wife" (Judges 21:21). [This occurred] during the event of the concubine in Gibe'ah.

Rabbi Shlomo Yitzchaki (Rashi)
1040–1105

Most noted biblical and Talmudic commentator. Born in Troyes, France, Rashi studied in the famed *yeshivot* of Mainz and Worms. His commentaries on the Pentateuch and the Talmud, which focus on the straightforward meaning of the text, appear in virtually every edition of the Talmud and Bible.

Concubine in Gibe'ah

TEXT 3

JUDGES 21:1–3

> א. וְאִישׁ יִשְׂרָאֵל נִשְׁבַּע בַּמִּצְפָּה לֵאמֹר, אִישׁ מִמֶּנּוּ לֹא יִתֵּן בִּתּוֹ לְבִנְיָמִן לְאִשָּׁה.
>
> ב. וַיָּבֹא הָעָם בֵּית אֵ-ל וַיֵּשְׁבוּ שָׁם עַד הָעֶרֶב לִפְנֵי הָאֱלֹקִים, וַיִּשְׂאוּ קוֹלָם וַיִּבְכּוּ בְּכִי גָדוֹל.
>
> ג. וַיֹּאמְרוּ לָמָה ה' אֱלֹקֵי יִשְׂרָאֵל הָיְתָה זֹאת בְּיִשְׂרָאֵל, לְהִפָּקֵד הַיּוֹם מִיִּשְׂרָאֵל שֵׁבֶט אֶחָד.

1. The men of Israel swore in Mizpah, saying, "No man among us will give his daughter to Benjamin for a wife."

2. The people came to Bethel and sat before G-d until the evening. They raised their voices and wept profusely.

3. And they said, "Why, O G-d, G-d of Israel, has this come to pass in Israel that one tribe of Israel should be missing today?"

Judges

Biblical book. The second book in the Prophets section of the Hebrew Bible, Judges relates the story of the early history of Jewish people in the Land of Israel. The era of the Judges (1228–931 BCE) was defined by tribalism and a repetitive cycle of anarchy and spiritual decay followed by national crisis, the rise of a strong leader, and return to G-d. The book was written by Samuel, who lived at the conclusion of the era of the Judges and guided the transition of the people toward a unified kingdom.

II. THE FOURTEEN-POINT SWING

The Pluck

TEXT 4

RASHI, GENESIS 49:27

> "בִּנְיָמִין זְאֵב יִטְרָף": זְאֵב הוּא אֲשֶׁר יִטְרָף.

"Benjamin, a preying wolf." Benjamin is a preying wolf.

TEXT 5

RASHI, GENESIS 8:11

> "טָרָף", חָטַף.

To prey means to snatch.

The Pluck of Gibeah

TEXT 6

THE REBBE, RABBI MENACHEM MENDEL SCHNEERSON,
TORAT MENACHEM 5744:2, P. 731

> לאחרי המאורע ד"פלגש בגבעה", מאורע בלתי רצוי לגמרי, היפך הקדושה בתכלית - לא היו יכולים להסתפק בעבודת הצדיקים "תמידים כסדרם", אלא היה הכרח בעבודת התשובה כדי לבטל את העניין הבלתי רצוי.
>
> ובודאי היתה עבודת התשובה בשלימותה (אצל אלה שנותרו משבט בנימין, לאחרי ביצוע העונש המגיע כו'), באופן של חרטה על העבר וקבלה טובה להבא, בריש גלי ובפירסום (שהכל ידעו שעלתה בידו לנצח את ה"א-ל זר אשר בקרבך", חלל השמאלי שבלב, ולהפכו לקדושה - בדוגמת הפירסום שהיה בעניין החטא, וכמאמר רבותינו זכרונם לברכה "באותו פרק באותו מקום").
>
> שלכן, חזר שבט בנימין להיבנות בשלימותו ולהיות בתוך כלל ישראל, כך שעל ידי זה חזרה השלימות דכלל ישראל.

Rabbi Menachem Mendel Schneerson 1902–1994

The towering Jewish leader of the 20th century, known as "the Lubavitcher Rebbe," or simply as "the Rebbe." Born in southern Ukraine, the Rebbe escaped Nazi-occupied Europe, arriving in the U.S. in June 1941. The Rebbe inspired and guided the revival of traditional Judaism after the European devastation, impacting virtually every Jewish community the world over. The Rebbe often emphasized that the performance of just one additional good deed could usher in the era of Mashiach. The Rebbe's scholarly talks and writings have been printed in more than 200 volumes.

The unfortunate, unholy episode of the concubine in Gibeah warranted genuine repentance. It was not enough to return to ordinary good behavior. It was necessary to cancel out the negative behavior.

The Benjaminites who survived the war repented wholeheartedly; they regretted their past and made positive resolutions for their future openly and publicly. As the entire nation knew of their sins, so did everyone know of their repentance. Everyone knew that they successfully overcame their sinful predilections and transformed them into merits.

This is why the tribe of Benjamin was completely restored and reinstated into the nation of Israel. Their repentance repaired the nation's integrity.

Catapulting Upward

TEXT 7

RABBI MENACHEM MENDEL OF LUBAVITCH, *OR HATORAH*, BERESHIT, P. 417A

> ועל כן נקרא "זאב יטרף", שטורף נפש הבהמית.
>
> ועל ידי זה טורף וממשיך מבחינה שלמעלה מהשתלשלות.

Benjamin is called a preying wolf because he preyed on his own beastly impulses.

By doing this, he snatched and drew down levels of holiness that were otherwise beyond his reach.

Rabbi Menachem Mendel of Lubavitch (*Tzemach Tzedek*) 1789–1866

Chasidic rebbe and noted author. The *Tzemach Tzedek* was the 3rd leader of the Chabad Chasidic movement and a noted authority on Jewish law. His numerous works include Halachic responsa, Chasidic discourses, and kabbalistic writings. Active in the communal affairs of Russian Jewry, he worked to alleviate the plight of the cantonists, Jewish children kidnapped to serve in the czar's army. He passed away in Lubavitch, leaving 7 sons and 2 daughters.

The Wife-Plucking

TEXT 8

THE REBBE, RABBI MENACHEM MENDEL SCHNEERSON,
TORAT MENACHEM 5744:2, P. 731

> ומכיון ששלימות ענין התשובה הוא לא רק ביטול הענין הבלתי רצוי מכל וכל, אלא גם העילוי דאתהפכא חשוכא לנהורא, הפיכת הדבר הבלתי רצוי גופא לקדושה - התבטא הדבר בענין החטיפה, "וחטפתם לכם איש אשתו" (שופטים כא, כא).
>
> מכיון שלא יכלו להסתפק בסדר הרגיל ד"כי יקח איש אשה", אלא היה צורך בהתגברות והתאמצות מיוחדת (חטיפה) בענין הנישואין, באופן של מהירות והיסח הדעת למעליותא.

In its most complete sense, repentance is not just canceling the negative but transforming that darkness to light. The undesirable behavior is transformed into holiness. Accordingly, they expressed repentance through plucking: "And each man must snatch his wife" (Judges 21:21).

The ordinary consent-seeking approach to marriage would not suffice for them. Their unique situation demanded an unusually intense and powerful "plucking" approach: one that is expressed through swiftness and transcendental absentmindedness.

III. NO CHALLENGE TOO GREAT

The Entire Nation

TEXT 9

TALMUD, MEGILAH 12A

> שָׁאֲלוּ תַּלְמִידָיו אֶת רַבִּי שִׁמְעוֹן בֶּן יוֹחַאי: מִפְּנֵי מָה נִתְחַיְּיבוּ שׂוֹנְאֵיהֶן שֶׁל יִשְׂרָאֵל שֶׁבְּאוֹתוֹ הַדּוֹר כְּלָיָה?
>
> אָמַר לָהֶם: אִמְרוּ אַתֶּם.
>
> אָמְרוּ לוֹ: מִפְּנֵי שֶׁנֶּהֱנוּ מִסְּעוּדָתוֹ שֶׁל אוֹתוֹ רָשָׁע.
>
> אִם כֵּן, שֶׁבְּשׁוּשָׁן יֵהָרְגוּ, שֶׁבְּכָל הָעוֹלָם כּוּלּוֹ אַל יֵהָרְגוּ?
>
> אָמְרוּ לוֹ, אֱמוֹר אַתָּה.
>
> אָמַר לָהֶם, מִפְּנֵי שֶׁהִשְׁתַּחֲווּ לַצֶּלֶם.

Babylonian Talmud

A literary work of monumental proportions that draws upon the legal, spiritual, intellectual, ethical, and historical traditions of Judaism. The 37 tractates of the Babylonian Talmud contain the teachings of the Jewish sages from the period after the destruction of the 2nd Temple through the 5th century CE. It has served as the primary vehicle for the transmission of the Oral Law and the education of Jews over the centuries; it is the entry point for all subsequent legal, ethical, and theological Jewish scholarship.

The students of Rabbi Shimon, son of Yocha'i, asked him, "Why were the enemies of the Jews in that generation deserving of annihilation?"

He said to them, "You answer."

They replied, "Because they partook of the feast of the wicked [Ahasuerus]."

[Rabbi Shimon responded,] "If so, only the Jews of Shushan [where the party took place] should have perished. The others should have been spared."

They said to him, "You answer your question."

He replied, "Because they bowed to an idol."

TEXT 10

RABBI SHNEUR ZALMAN OF LIADI, *TORAH OR*, P. 97A

> אם רצו להמיר דתם לא היה המן עושה להם כלום, שלא גזר אלא על היהודים. אלא שהם מסרו עצמן למות כל השנה כולה, ולא עלה להם מחשבת חוץ, חס ושלום.
>
> ועל ידי בחינת מסירת נפש, זכו.

Had they chosen to abandon their faith, Haman would not have harmed them, for his decree was only against Jews. Nevertheless, they risked their lives for an entire year. The possibility of apostasy never even occurred to them, G-d forbid.

They merited [their salvation] on account of their self-sacrifice.

Rabbi Shneur Zalman of Liadi (Alter Rebbe)
1745–1812

Chasidic rebbe, Halachic authority, and founder of the Chabad movement. The Alter Rebbe was born in Liozna, Belarus, and was among the principal students of the Magid of Mezeritch. His numerous works include the *Tanya*, an early classic containing the fundamentals of Chabad Chasidism; and *Shulchan Aruch HaRav,* an expanded and reworked code of Jewish law.

TEXT 11

RABBI YAAKOV KATINA, *KORBAN HAANI* ON PURIM

> מובא בשם הרוקח, שפירוש "ועת צרה היא ליעקב וממנה יושע" (ירמיה ל, ז), "וממנה" אותיות "ומהמן", כי על ידו באה לנו הישועה.
>
> כי היו על ישראל ב' חטאים, שהשתחוו לצלם בימי נבוכדנצר, ושנהנו מסעודתו של אותו רשע. והיה עליהם קטרוג גדול, "ועת צרה היא ליעקב". ועל ידי גזירת המן, עשו תשובה . . .
>
> ועל ידי תשובה זו, נתעלו ישראל ברום המעלות, הן למעלה והן למטה.

Rabbi Yaakov Katina
d. 1890

Halachic authority. A student of Rabbi Chaim Halberstam of Sanz and other Chasidic rabbis in the Ukraine/Poland area, Rabbi Yaakov Katina served as a Halachic authority in Khust, Ukraine, for 40 years. He is best known for his collection of insights on the Torah titled *Korban Haani*, and for the lengthy ethical will he wrote for his family, *Rachamei Haav*.

[The prophet said] "It was a time of distress for Jacob, and from it he will be saved" (Jeremiah 30:7). The following interpretation is brought in the name of Rabbi Eliezer of Worms, author of *Sefer Roke'ach*. In Hebrew, the words "from it—*umimenah*" can be rearranged as an anagram to read "*umiHaman*—and from Haman." The message is that Haman brought about our salvation.

The Jewish people were guilty of two sins: (a) They bowed to an idol in the era of Nebuchadnezzar, and (b) they partook of the evil one's feast. A terrible fate was decreed upon them [in Heaven]; "it was a time of distress for Jacob." However, when Haman promulgated his decree, the Jews were inspired to repentance.

And it was this repentance that catapulted them to great heights both in Heaven and on earth.

Conclusion

TEXT 12A

RABBI SHMUEL SCHNEERSON OF LUBAVITCH, CITED IN *TORAT MENACHEM* 5782:3, P. 1396

> די וועלט זאגט, אז אויב מ'קען ניט ארונטער גייט מען אריבער. און איך זאג, אז מ'דארף גיין לכתחילה אריבער.

The world says that if you can't wiggle past underneath, climb over the top. I say go directly over the top.

Rabbi Shmuel Schneersohn (Rebbe Maharash)
1834–1882

Known by the acronym "Maharash"; 4th Chabad rebbe and leader of Russian Jewry. Born in Lubavitch, Russia, he was the youngest son of Rabbi Menachem Mendel of Lubavitch (the *Tzemach Tzedek*). Much of his leadership was devoted to combating anti-Jewish policies. His discourses have been collected and published as *Likutei Torah: Torat Shmuel*.

TEXT 12B

TALMUD, ERUVIN 54A

> אָמַר לֵיהּ שְׁמוּאֵל לְרַב יְהוּדָה: שִׁינָּנָא, חֲטוֹף וֶאֱכוֹל חֲטוֹף וְאִישְׁתִּי, דְעָלְמָא דְּאָזְלִינַן מִינֵּיהּ כְּהִלּוּלָא דָּמֵי.

Rabbi Shmuel said to [his student] Rabbi Yehudah, "Well-versed one, grab and eat, grab and drink, for this world we will [soon] depart from is like a wedding."

TEXT 12C

RABBI SHALOM DOVBER SCHNEERSOHN, INTRODUCTION TO *KUNTRES UMAAYAN*, P. 22

> מה שכותב כבודו, אבל אנו מה כחינו. זאת לא אוכל לקבל בשום אופן.
>
> כחינו רב הוא . . .
>
> ולדעתי, לפי שעתה הוא זמן הבירורים היותר אחרונים דעקבות משיחא, וכאשר למשל קדירה בגמר בישולה היא רותחת ביותר, ובעת הרתיחה, מה שבשולי הקדירה עולה למעלה כו'. כמו כן בתוקף הבירורים בזמן האחרון, הנה כמה דברים שנראים לנו על פי שכל רחוק מאד שיתוקן, יכול להיות שהוא קרוב לגמרי . . .
>
> ולכן אנחנו מצדינו, אין אנו יכולים, וגם אין רשאים, בזמן הזה בפרט לברר מה שקרוב או רחוק על פי שכלנו. כל אחד מה שאנו מוצאים שצריך תיקון, צריכים אנחנו להשתדל בכחות עצומות, וה' יתברך יעשה את שלו, ויהיה בעזרינו.

Rabbi Shalom Dovber Schneersohn (Rashab)
1860–1920

Chasidic rebbe. Rabbi Shalom Dovber became the 5th leader of the Chabad movement upon the passing of his father, Rabbi Shmuel Schneersohn. He established the Lubavitch network of *yeshivot* called Tomchei Temimim. He authored many volumes of Chasidic discourses and is renowned for his lucid and thorough explanations of kabbalistic concepts.

You wrote that we lack the strength [to accomplish this task]. This I cannot accept under any circumstances.

We have extraordinary strength. . . .

Poised as we are for the coming of Mashiach, we are now completing the final tasks of our Exile. In my opinion, it is like a pot. When a pot boils over, the food on the bottom rises to the top. We are like that boiling pot. Even tasks that appear impossible are eminently doable. . . .

Therefore, we cannot and must not act on the basis of what we believe is possible. We must take on every challenge we encounter and give it everything we have. And G-d will do His part and assist us.

KEY POINTS

» The ordinary way to worship G-d is to be righteous—avoid all sin and observe all the *mitzvot*.

» A person who adopts a path of sin, especially heinous sin, is not expected to become a worshipper of G-d. Yet, such people can surprise us and snatch victory from their sins. They can repent and reach a more desirable state than those who have never sinned.

» Jacob blessed his son Benjamin to be like a preying wolf. As a wolf snatches what is not meant to belong to it, so do penitents snatch their sins and turn them into merits.

» The moral is that no challenge is too daunting. Every challenge is given to us by G-d in the belief that we are capable of overcoming it. We must never shy away from a challenge. If it is placed before us, it was meant for us to overcome and turn what could have been a terrible liability into a powerful asset.

» If this is true of challenges that result from our sins, it is certainly true of challenges that come our way when we are in a state of righteousness and spiritual integrity.

12.
Shemot

The Ideal Jew
Hint: It's Not a Rabbi

Dedicated to Jack and Judy Miller in appreciation for their friendship and partnership with JLI and their dedication to bringing the light of Torah to communities across the globe

PARSHAH OVERVIEW
Shemot

The Children of Israel multiply in Egypt. Threatened by their growing numbers, Pharaoh enslaves them and orders the Hebrew midwives, Shifrah and Pu'ah, to kill all male babies at birth. When they do not comply, he commands his people to cast the Hebrew babies into the Nile.

A child is born to Jochebed—the daughter of Levi—and her husband, Amram. This baby is placed in a basket on the river, while the baby's sister, Miriam, stands watch from afar. Pharaoh's daughter discovers the boy, raises him as her son, and names him Moses.

As a young man, Moses leaves the palace and discovers the hardship of his people. He sees an Egyptian beating a Hebrew and kills the Egyptian. The next day, he sees two Jews fighting; when he admonishes them, they reveal his deed of the previous day, and Moses is forced to flee to Midian. There, he rescues Jethro's daughters, marries one of them (Zipporah), and becomes a shepherd of his father-in-law's flocks.

G-d appears to Moses in a Burning Bush at the foot of Mount Sinai and instructs him to go to Pharaoh and demand, "Let My people go, so that they may serve Me." Moses's brother, Aaron, is appointed to serve as his spokesman. In Egypt, Moses and Aaron assemble the elders of Israel to tell them that the time of their redemption has come. The people believe them, but Pharaoh refuses to let them go and even intensifies the suffering of Israel.

Moses returns to G-d to protest, "Why have You done evil to this people?" G-d promises that their redemption is close at hand.

INTRODUCTION

The rules that we will use to analyze Rashi's approach:

1. When Rashi cites the source for his comment, he does it to answer a question or provide support for his comment on the verse. For this reason, Rashi doesn't typically cite his source.

2. Rashi's commentary—*peshat*—favors action over emotion. It values what we do more than what we achieve emotionally or psychologically.

3. The language the Torah uses plays an integral part in the plain meaning of the text. It compels Rashi to give his explanation over another's even if the other explanation is simpler in other ways.

4. The plain meaning of the text doesn't always mean the most literal interpretation of the text; it means the simplest and most straightforward understanding of the text *in context*. This may lead Rashi to choose a less literal but more contextually appropriate interpretation.

Question for Discussion

What is the greatest form of Jewish nachas? What is the surest way to guarantee Jewish continuity?

I. DEFIANCE AND REWARD

Heroic Defiance

TEXT 1

EXODUS 1:15–19

> טו. וַיֹּאמֶר מֶלֶךְ מִצְרַיִם לַמְיַלְּדֹת הָעִבְרִיֹּת, אֲשֶׁר שֵׁם הָאַחַת שִׁפְרָה וְשֵׁם הַשֵּׁנִית פּוּעָה.
>
> טז. וַיֹּאמֶר, בְּיַלֶּדְכֶן אֶת הָעִבְרִיּוֹת וּרְאִיתֶן עַל הָאָבְנָיִם, אִם בֵּן הוּא וַהֲמִתֶּן אֹתוֹ וְאִם בַּת הִיא וָחָיָה.
>
> יז. וַתִּירֶאןָ הַמְיַלְּדֹת אֶת הָאֱלֹקִים וְלֹא עָשׂוּ כַּאֲשֶׁר דִּבֶּר אֲלֵיהֶן מֶלֶךְ מִצְרָיִם, וַתְּחַיֶּיןָ אֶת הַיְלָדִים.
>
> יח. וַיִּקְרָא מֶלֶךְ מִצְרַיִם לַמְיַלְּדֹת, וַיֹּאמֶר לָהֶן, מַדּוּעַ עֲשִׂיתֶן הַדָּבָר הַזֶּה וַתְּחַיֶּיןָ אֶת הַיְלָדִים.
>
> יט. וַתֹּאמַרְןָ הַמְיַלְּדֹת אֶל פַּרְעֹה, כִּי לֹא כַנָּשִׁים הַמִּצְרִיֹּת הָעִבְרִיֹּת כִּי חָיוֹת הֵנָּה, בְּטֶרֶם תָּבוֹא אֲלֵהֶן הַמְיַלֶּדֶת וְיָלָדוּ.

15. The king of Egypt spoke to the Hebrew midwives, one of whom was named Shifrah and the other Pu'ah.

16. And he said, "When you deliver the Hebrew women, look at the birth stool: if it is a boy, kill him; if it is a girl, let her live."

17. The midwives, fearing G-d, did not do as the king of Egypt had told them; they let the boys live.

18. So the king of Egypt summoned the midwives and said to them, "Why have you done this thing, letting the boys live?"

19. The midwives said to Pharaoh, "Because the Hebrew women are not like the Egyptian women: They are vigorous. Before the midwife can come to them, they have given birth."

The Reward

TEXT 2

EXODUS 1:20-21

> כ. וַיֵּיטֶב אֱלֹקִים לַמְיַלְּדֹת, וַיִּרֶב הָעָם וַיַּעַצְמוּ מְאֹד.
>
> כא. וַיְהִי כִּי יָרְאוּ הַמְיַלְּדֹת אֶת הָאֱלֹקִים, וַיַּעַשׂ לָהֶם בָּתִּים.

20. And G-d dealt well with the midwives; and the people multiplied and increased greatly.

21. And because the midwives feared G-d, He made them houses.

TEXT 3

RASHI, EXODUS 1:21

> "וַיַּעַשׂ לָהֶם בָּתִּים". בָּתֵּי כְּהֻנָּה וּלְוִיָּה וּמַלְכוּת שֶׁקְּרוּיִין בָּתִּים, כְּמוֹ שֶׁכָּתוּב: "לִבְנוֹת אֶת בֵּית ה' וְאֶת בֵּית הַמֶּלֶךְ" (מלכים א ט, א), כְּהֻנָּה וּלְוִיָּה מִיּוֹכֶבֶד, וּמַלְכוּת מִמִּרְיָם. כִּדְאִיתָא בְּמַסֶּכֶת סוֹטָה.

Rabbi Shlomo Yitzchaki (Rashi)
1040–1105

Most noted biblical and Talmudic commentator. Born in Troyes, France, Rashi studied in the famed *yeshivot* of Mainz and Worms. His commentaries on the Pentateuch and the Talmud, which focus on the straightforward meaning of the text, appear in virtually every edition of the Talmud and Bible.

"He made them houses." Houses [dynasties] of the priesthood and of the Levites and of royalty, which are all termed בתים, "houses," as the verse states, "And Solomon built the House of G-d and the house of the king" (I Kings 9:1). "The House of G-d," i.e., a dynasty of priests and Levites from Jochebed [Shifrah]; and "the house of the king," i.e., a royal dynasty from Miriam [Pu'ah], just as it is stated in the Talmud, Tractate Sotah.

Questions on Rashi

TEXT 4

TALMUD, SOTAH 11B

> "וַיְהִי כִּי יָרְאוּ הַמְיַלְּדֹת אֶת הָאֱלֹקִים וַיַּעַשׂ לָהֶם בָּתִּים".
>
> רַב וּשְׁמוּאֵל. חַד אָמַר: בָּתֵּי כְהוּנָּה וּלְוִיָּה, וְחַד אָמַר: בָּתֵּי מַלְכוּת.
>
> מַאן דְּאָמַר בָּתֵּי כְהוּנָּה וּלְוִיָּה – אַהֲרֹן וּמֹשֶׁה.
>
> וּמַאן דְּאָמַר בָּתֵּי מַלְכוּת – דָּוִד נַמִי מִמִּרְיָם קָאָתֵי.

"And it came to pass, because the midwives feared G-d, He made them houses" (Exodus 1:21).

Rav and Shmuel disagree as to the precise interpretation of these houses: One says that G-d made the houses of the priesthood and the Levites descend from the midwives, and one says that G-d made the houses of royalty descend from them.

The one who says that it is referring to the houses of the priesthood and the Levites is referring to Aaron and Moses, who were sons of Jochebed.

And the one who says that it is referring to houses of royalty is referring to David, who also comes from Miriam.

Babylonian Talmud

A literary work of monumental proportions that draws upon the legal, spiritual, intellectual, ethical, and historical traditions of Judaism. The 37 tractates of the Babylonian Talmud contain the teachings of the Jewish sages from the period after the destruction of the 2nd Temple through the 5th century CE. It has served as the primary vehicle for the transmission of the Oral Law and the education of Jews over the centuries; it is the entry point for all subsequent legal, ethical, and theological Jewish scholarship.

TEXT 5

MIDRASH, *SHEMOT RABAH* 1:16

דָּבָר אַחֵר, "וַיֵּיטֶב אֱלֹקִים", אָמַר רַבִּי בֶּרֶכְיָה בְּשֵׁם רַבִּי חִיָּא בֶּן רַבִּי אַבָּא: הֲדָא הוּא דִכְתִיב (אִיּוֹב כח, כח) "וַיֹּאמֶר לָאָדָם הֵן יִרְאַת ה' הִיא חָכְמָה", מַהוּ שְׂכַר הַיִּרְאָה? תּוֹרָה.

לְפִי שֶׁיִּרְאָה יוֹכֶבֶד מִפְּנֵי הַקָּדוֹשׁ בָּרוּךְ הוּא - הֶעֱמִיד מִמֶּנָּה מֹשֶׁה, שֶׁכָּתוּב בּוֹ (שְׁמוֹת ב, ב) "כִּי טוֹב הוּא" וְנִתְּנָה הַתּוֹרָה עַל יָדוֹ, שֶׁנִּקְרֵאת (מִשְׁלֵי ד, ב) "לֶקַח טוֹב", וְנִקְרֵאת עַל שְׁמוֹ, שֶׁנֶּאֱמַר (מַלְאָכִי ג, כב) "זִכְרוּ תּוֹרַת מֹשֶׁה עַבְדִּי".

וּמִרְיָם, יָצָא מִמֶּנָּה בְּצַלְאֵל שֶׁהָיָה מָלֵא חָכְמָה, דִּכְתִיב (שְׁמוֹת לא, ג) "וָאֲמַלֵּא אֹתוֹ רוּחַ אֱלֹקִים וְגוֹ'". וְעָשָׂה אָרוֹן לַתּוֹרָה שֶׁנִּקְרֵאת טוֹב, הֱוֵי: "וַיֵּיטֶב אֱלֹקִים לַמְיַלְּדֹת".

Shemot Rabah

An early rabbinic commentary on the Book of Exodus. "Midrash" is the designation of a particular genre of rabbinic literature usually forming a running commentary on specific books of the Bible. *Shemot Rabah*, written mostly in Hebrew, provides textual exegeses, expounds upon the biblical narrative, and develops and illustrates moral principles. It was first printed in Constantinople in 1512 together with 4 other Midrashic works on the other 4 books of the Pentateuch.

"G-d dealt well with the midwives." Rabbi Berechya said in the name of Rabbi Chiya ben Rabbi Abba: That is what is written, "He said to man: Behold, fear of G-d that is wisdom" (Job 28:28). What is the reward for fear? It is Torah.

Because Jochebed feared G-d, she begot Moses, of whom it is written, "he was good" (Exodus 2:2). And the Torah, which is also called "a good acquisition" (Proverbs 4:2), was given through him, and is called after his name, as it is stated, "Remember the Torah of Moses My servant" (Malachi 3:22).

As for Miriam, Bezalel, who was filled with wisdom, as it is written, "I filled him with the spirit of G-d [with wisdom]" (Exodus 31:3), emerged from her. And he crafted an ark for the Torah, which is called "good"—that is: "G-d was good to the midwives."

II. A FITTING REWARD

Literal Houses

TEXT 6A

RABBI AVRAHAM IBN EZRA, *PIRUSH HAKATZAR L'IBN EZRA*

> וַיֹּאמַר הַגָּאוֹן, כִּי עָשָׂה לָהֶם בָּתִּים שֶׁהִסְתִּירָם שָׁם וְלֹא נִמְצָאוּ.

The Ga'on explained: He made them houses, where they hid (from Pharaoh) and were not found.

Rabbi Avraham ibn Ezra
1092–1167

Biblical commentator, linguist, and poet. Ibn Ezra was born in Toledo, Spain, and fled the Almohad regime to other parts of Europe. It is believed that he was living in London at the time of his death. Ibn Ezra is best known for his literalistic commentary on the Pentateuch. He also wrote works of poetry, philosophy, medicine, astronomy, and other topics.

TEXT 6B

RABBI DAVID KIMCHI, *SEFER SHORASHIM, SHORASH BATIM*

> והנראה בעיני כי פירוש "ויעש להם בתים", שהסתירם מפרעה שלא הרע להם.

The interpretation of the verse "G-d made them houses" is that G-d hid them from Pharaoh so that he should not do them any harm.

Rabbi David Kimchi (Radak)
1160–1235

Provençal medieval grammarian and biblical exegete. Rabbi Kimchi wrote a comprehensive exposition of Hebrew grammar called *Miklol*; and *Sefer Hashorashim*, a dictionary of the Bible.

Rashi Rule #2

TEXT 7

TALMUD, SOTAH 8B

> בְּמִדָּה שֶׁאָדָם מוֹדֵד – בָּהּ מוֹדְדִין לוֹ.

A person is rewarded according to the magnitude of their action.

TEXT 8

MISHNAH, SOTAH 1:9

> וְכֵן לְעִנְיַן הַטּוֹבָה: מִרְיָם הִמְתִּינָה לְמֹשֶׁה שָׁעָה אַחַת, שֶׁנֶּאֱמַר (שְׁמוֹת ב, ד) "וַתֵּתַצַּב אֲחֹתוֹ מֵרָחֹק", לְפִיכָךְ נִתְעַכְּבוּ לָהּ יִשְׂרָאֵל שִׁבְעָה יָמִים בַּמִּדְבָּר, שֶׁנֶּאֱמַר (בַּמִּדְבָּר יב, טו) "וְהָעָם לֹא נָסַע עַד הֵאָסֵף מִרְיָם".

A person is rewarded "measure for measure" for their good deeds. Miriam waited for Moses for one hour at the shore of the Nile, as it is stated: "And his sister stood far off, to know what would be done to him" (Exodus 2:4). Therefore, the Jewish people delayed their travels in the desert for seven days to wait for her when she had leprosy, as it is stated, "And Miriam was confined outside of the camp for seven days; and the people journeyed not until Miriam was brought in again" (Numbers 12:15).

Mishnah

The first authoritative work of Jewish law that was codified in writing. The Mishnah contains the oral traditions that were passed down from teacher to student; it supplements, clarifies, and systematizes the commandments of the Torah. Due to the continual persecution of the Jewish people, it became increasingly difficult to guarantee that these traditions would not be forgotten. Rabbi Yehudah Hanasi therefore redacted the Mishnah at the end of the 2nd century. It serves as the foundation for the Talmud.

The True Accomplishment of the Midwives

TEXT 9A

RABBI YOSEF CHAIM OF BAGHDAD, *BEN YEHOYADA*, SOTAH 11B

> ונראה נתן להם זה מדה כנגד מדה: הם חסו על כללות ישראל, לכך נתן כתר כהונה וכתר מלכות, אשר בשתיים אלה תלוי כללות כל ישראל.

To explain how G-d rewarded them measure for measure: they were concerned for the entire nation; therefore, G-d gave them the crown of priesthood and the crown of kingship, upon which the entire nation is hinged.

Rabbi Yosef Chaim of Baghdad (*Ben Ish Chai*)
1834–1909

Sefardic Halachist and kabbalist. Rabbi Yosef Chaim succeeded his father as chief rabbi of Baghdad in 1859, and is best known as author of his Halachic work, *Ben Ish Chai*, by which title he is also known. Also popular is his commentary on the homiletical sections of the Talmud, called *Ben Yehoyada*.

TEXT 9B

THE REBBE, RABBI MENACHEM MENDEL SCHNEERSON, *LIKUTEI SICHOT* 21, P. 6

> די פעולה פון די מיילדות אין דעם וואס "ותחיינה את הלדים" איז געווען ניט נאר דאס וואס זיי האבן דורכדעם געהאלפן אז עס זאלן אויפגעשטעלט ווערן אידישע משפחות, נאר דורך דעם האט זיך אויפגעשטעלט דער (רוב, אדער) גאנצער דור יוצאי מצרים פון וועמען ס'קומט ארויס דער גאנצער עם ישראל עד סוף כל הדורות.
>
> און דעריבער איז דער שכר באופן דמדה כנגד מדה ובפרטיות, ניט דאס וואס זיי האבן געהאט בנים ומשפחות, אדער אז זיי האבן געהאט קינדער כהנים לוים ומלכים, נאר פון זיי זיינען אויפגעבויט געווארן "בתי כהונה ולויה ומלכות", די בתים מיוחדים, "יתר שאת ויתר עז" שבישראל עד סוף כל הדורות.

The accomplishment of the midwives wasn't limited to saving Jewish boys and families alone; they were responsible for saving pretty much the entire generation that left Egypt, the progenitors for all subsequent Jewish generations.

G-d rewarded them in kind: The reward wasn't limited to their own personal families. Rather, they became the ancestors of the "houses of *Kohanim*, *Leviim*, and royalty." They spawned the unique dynasties of Israel for all future generations.

Rabbi Menachem Mendel Schneerson
1902–1994

The towering Jewish leader of the 20th century, known as "the Lubavitcher Rebbe," or simply as "the Rebbe." Born in southern Ukraine, the Rebbe escaped Nazi-occupied Europe, arriving in the U.S. in June 1941. The Rebbe inspired and guided the revival of traditional Judaism after the European devastation, impacting virtually every Jewish community the world over. The Rebbe often emphasized that the performance of just one additional good deed could usher in the era of Mashiach. The Rebbe's scholarly talks and writings have been printed in more than 200 volumes.

Reexamining the Midrash's Interpretation

TEXT 10

DEUTERONOMY 6:24

> וַיְצַוֵּנוּ ה׳ לַעֲשׂוֹת אֶת כָּל הַחֻקִּים הָאֵלֶּה, לְיִרְאָה אֶת ה׳ אֱלֹקֵינוּ, לְטוֹב לָנוּ כָּל הַיָּמִים, לְחַיֹּתֵנוּ כְּהַיּוֹם הַזֶּה.

And G-d commanded us to do all these statutes, to *fear* the L-rd our G-d, for our *good* always, that He might preserve us alive, as it is at this day.

III. RASHI'S PRACTICAL FOCUS

Talmud vs. Midrash: Distinguishing the Works

TEXT 11

THE REBBE, RABBI MENACHEM MENDEL SCHNEERSON, *HAYOM YOM*, 16 TEVET

> דער צמח צדק האט געזאגט ר' הענדל'ן אויף יחידות: זוהר אין מרומם דעם נפש, מדרש איז מעורר דאס הארץ, און תהלים מיט טרערען וואשט אויס די כלי.

The *Tzemach Tzedek* told Reb Hendel in a private audience: "*Zohar* uplifts the soul, Midrash inspires the heart, Psalms with tears cleanses the vessel."

Rashi Rule #3

TEXT 12

THE REBBE, RABBI MENACHEM MENDEL SCHNEERSON, *LIKUTEI SICHOT* 21, P. 8

> און פירוש רש"י, פשוטו של מקרא, וואס איז פארבונדן מיט עשיה ממש . . . הערט זיך אן אז "לא המדרש עיקר אלא המעשה", די מעשה בפועל . . .
>
> דעריבער איז דא נוגע דער שכר פון בתי כהונה ולויה ומלכות, און פארבונדן אויך מיט "את בית ה' ואת בית המלך", בתים כפשוטו בגשמיות, ווייל זייער עיקר מעלה און אויפטו איז געווען דאס וואס זיי האבן אויפגעשטעלט און תחיינה - לעבעדיק געמאכט בתים בישראל.

Rashi's commentary, explaining the plain meaning of the text, is connected to the world of action. Its concern is reflected in the statement, "Exegesis is not the main point, but rather action" (Mishnah, Avot 1:17) is the bottom line. . . .

As such, the relevant reward here is the houses of *Kohanim*, *Leviim*, and royalty, which are also connected to actual homes, "the House of G-d and the house of the king," because the most crucial element was their *actions*—namely, sparing and preserving the eternal Jewish home.

IV. DEFINING A SUCCESSFUL JEW

TEXT 13

MAIMONIDES, *MISHNEH TORAH*, LAWS OF *SHEMITAH* AND *YOVEL* 13:12–13

> וְלֹא שֵׁבֶט לֵוִי בִּלְבַד, אֶלָּא כָּל אִישׁ וְאִישׁ מִכָּל בָּאֵי הָעוֹלָם אֲשֶׁר נָדְבָה רוּחוֹ אוֹתוֹ וֶהֱבִינוֹ מַדָּעוֹ לְהִבָּדֵל לַעֲמֹד לִפְנֵי ה' לְשָׁרְתוֹ וּלְעָבְדוֹ לְדֵעָה אֶת ה', וְהָלַךְ יָשָׁר כְּמוֹ שֶׁעֲשָׂהוּ הָאֱלֹקִים . . . וְיִהְיֶה ה' חֶלְקוֹ וְנַחֲלָתוֹ לְעוֹלָם וּלְעוֹלְמֵי עוֹלָמִים.

Not only the tribe of Levi, but any human being whose spirit and understanding motivates them to dedicate themselves to the service and knowledge of G-d, and walks justly as G-d made them. . . . G-d will be their portion and heritage forever.

Rabbi Moshe ben Maimon (Maimonides, Rambam)
1135–1204

Halachist, philosopher, author, and physician. Maimonides was born in Córdoba, Spain. After the conquest of Córdoba by the Almohads, he fled Spain and eventually settled in Cairo, Egypt. There, he became the leader of the Jewish community and served as court physician to the vizier of Egypt. He is most noted for authoring the *Mishneh Torah*, an encyclopedic arrangement of Jewish law; and for his philosophical work, *Guide for the Perplexed*. His rulings on Jewish law are integral to the formation of Halachic consensus.

TEXT 14

TALMUD, BERACHOT 58A

> דמלכותא דארעא כעין מלכותא דרקיעא.

Human royalty mirrors Heavenly royalty.

KEY POINTS

» Jewish success and continuity are about active Jewish engagement and helping others engage, not just intellectual achievements.

» Jochebed and Miriam saved Hebrew boys, preserving the future of the Jewish nation.

» G-d rewarded the midwives with dynasties of *Kohanim*, *Leviim*, and royalty, reflecting their role in ensuring Jewish continuity.

» Rashi's interpretation emphasizes action and practical outcomes over intellectual and emotional achievements.

» Jewish parents and educators should raise children who actively engage in their Jewish identity and inspire others, ensuring the strength and continuity of the Jewish people.

THE ROHR
Jewish Learning Institute

832 Eastern Parkway, Brooklyn, New York 11213

CHAIRMAN
Rabbi Moshe Kotlarsky, OBM

PRINCIPAL BENEFACTOR
Mr. George Rohr
New York, NY

EXECUTIVE DIRECTOR
Rabbi Efraim Mintz

ADMINISTRATION
Rabbi Mendel Kotlarsky

ADMINISTRATOR
Rabbi Dubi Rabinowitz

EXECUTIVE COMMITTEE
Rabbi Chaim Block
S. Antonio, TX
Rabbi Hesh Epstein
Columbia, SC
Rabbi Ronnie Fine
Montreal, Quebec
Rabbi Yosef Gansburg
Toronto, Ontario
Rabbi Shmuel Kaplan
Potomac, MD
Rabbi Yisrael Rice
S. Rafael, CA
Rabbi Avrohom Sternberg
New London, CT

TORAH STUDIES

CHAIRMAN
Rabbi Yosef Gansburg
Toronto, Ontario

EDITOR
Rabbi Ahrele Loschak
Brooklyn, NY

CONTRIBUTING AUTHOR
Rabbi Eliezer Gurkow
London, ON

ADMINISTRATOR
Rabbi Shlomie Tenenbaum
Brooklyn, NY

FOUNDING DIRECTOR
Rabbi Meir Hecht
Chicago, IL

STEERING COMMITTEE
Rabbi Levi Fogelman
Natick, MA
Rabbi Yaakov Halperin
Allentown, PA
Rabbi Nechemiah Schusterman
Peabody, MA
Rabbi Ari Sollish
Atlanta, GA

CONTENT EDITORS
Rabbi Mendel Brawer
Brooklyn, NY
Rabbi Eliezer Gurkow
London, ON

TEXTBOOK LAYOUT
Rabbi Motti Klein
Rabbi Moshe Wolff

GRAPHIC DESIGN
Mrs. Chaya Mushka Kanner
Mrs. Chaya Katz
Mrs. Estie Klein

SENIOR PROOFREADERS
Mrs. Rachel Musicante
Silver Springs, MD
Mrs. Ya'akovah Weber
Brooklyn, NY

PROOFREADER
Ms. Mimi Palace
Brooklyn, NY

COPY EDITING
Mr. Michael Barnett
Bel Air, MD

POWERPOINT PRESENTATIONS
Ms. Chaya Barnett
Brooklyn, NY
Mrs. Chana Zajac
Brooklyn, NY

PUBLICATION AND DISTRIBUTION
Rabbi Moshe Raichik
Brooklyn, NY
Rabbi Mendel Sirota
Brooklyn, NY

An affiliate of
Merkos L'Inyonei Chinuch
The Education Arm of the Worldwide Chabad-Lubavitch Movement

The Jewish Learning Multiplex

Brought to you by the Rohr Jewish Learning Institute

In fulfillment of the mandate of the Lubavitcher Rebbe, of blessed memory, whose leadership guides every step of our work, the mission of the Rohr Jewish Learning Institute is to transform Jewish life and the greater community through the study of Torah, connecting each Jew to our shared heritage of Jewish learning.

While our flagship program remains the cornerstone of our organization, JLI is proud to feature additional divisions catering to specific populations, in order to meet a wide array of educational needs.

THE ROHR JEWISH LEARNING INSTITUTE

A subsidiary of Merkos L'Inyonei Chinuch,
the adult education arm of the Chabad-Lubavitch movement

Torah Studies provides a rich and nuanced encounter with the weekly Torah reading.

JLI Teens — Jewish teens forge their identity as they engage in Torah study, social interaction, and serious fun.

Rosh Chodesh Society gathers Jewish women together once a month for intensive textual study.

TorahCafe.com provides an exclusive selection of top-rated Jewish educational videos.

The Land & The Spirit — JLI Israel Experience — Participants delve into our nation's past while exploring the Holy Land's relevance and meaning today.

National Jewish Retreat — This yearly event rejuvenates mind, body, and spirit with a powerful synthesis of Jewish learning and community.

The Wellness Institute equips youths facing adulthood with education and resources to address youth mental health.

JLI Academy — Select affiliates are invited to partner with peers and noted professionals, as leaders of innovation and excellence.

MyShiur — Talmud Learning Initiative — MyShiur courses are designed to assist students in developing the skills needed to study Talmud independently.

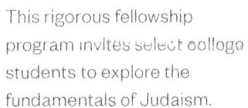

Sinai Scholars Society — This rigorous fellowship program invites select college students to explore the fundamentals of Judaism.

RIIH — Read It In Hebrew — A crash course that teaches adults to read Hebrew in just five sessions.

Machon Shmuel — The Sami Rohr Research Institute is an institute providing Torah research in the service of educators worldwide.

Printed in Great Britain
by Amazon